"I have known and admired Bob Ricker since we were teenagers. Over the years, he has demonstrated a deep love for people. This book is an expression of that love as he addresses the subject of doubt which is experienced by so many people. I encourage you to read it carefully. I believe that God will use it to help you overcome any doubts you may be experiencing including doubts about your eternal destination."

Dr. Paul Cedar,
Chairman/CEO of Mission America Coalition

"*Assured of Heaven* is an outstanding work on a much-needed subject. It will be a great help to those who struggle with doubts about their salvation. Dr. Ricker does a masterful job of explaining biblical texts and their impact on understanding salvation. In *Assured of Heaven* he tells of his own pilgrimage from childhood doubts to childlike faith. He is a blessing to our church and his new book, *Assured of Heaven,* will be a blessing to every church, pastor, and individual who reads it."

Dr. Dan Borg, Senior Pastor,
Bethany Church on the Hill, Thousand Oaks, California

"This is without doubt the most comprehensive work I have seen on the assurance of salvation. Bob has gone to great depths of analysis and observation, and all with solid scriptural support!"

Dr. John A. Anderson, Pastor and Church Leader

"Faith and doubt coexist in our lives as spiritual beings created in God's image but we are finite and fallen too. Dr. Ricker is a reliable and helpful guide through the thicket of tensions we experience as we seek confidence and assurance regarding our destiny. Dr. Ricker, through his own story, gives us permission to face our questions and doubts as we seek assurance and confidence in the faith commitments we have made to the Lord. This book is a good guide for us as we live in the tension of the search for assurance, confidence, and certitude."

Dr. George Brushaber,
President Emeritus of Bethel University

"Most thoughtful Christians at one time or another encounter doubt about the essentials of faith. Bob Ricker, from his own faith journey, encourages readers to own these doubts. He further provides helpful, biblical answers for working through the maze. You will see his convictions about certain doctrinal issues, including some that are much debated, but at the same time he is congenial toward those of other persuasions. The spirit of conciliation permeates his writing. Helpful discussion questions make it a good study resource for group or individual work. I recommend this book with enthusiasm."

Dr. David Rambo,
former President of Nyack College and Seminary,
former President of the Christian and Missionary Alliance

Endorsements

bios and additional information on endorsers
available at www.assurancebooks.com

"Dr. Ricker's new book, *Assured of Heaven*, clearly addresses the deepest anxiety of the human heart: Can I be certain of going to heaven? He persuasively and decisively answers with a resounding 'Yes!' In simple but profound words, he covers the subject with sensitivity and deftness. I have known Bob for more than 20 years—not just for his role as leader of one of America's most evangelical church denominations. I have come to know both he and his wife, Dee, as close and encouraging friends. His power as a preacher is now manifest in the skill he uses in writing this book. Having experienced his pastoral care during a tragic death in my own family, I see that same compassion on every page of this book. He does not hesitate to share his own journey. This book is most helpful both for pre-Christians and new Christians. But it calls all of us who have been Christians for some time; whether we be pastors, theologians, apologists, or leaders—we will find ourselves called to return to our first love and certainty—that we are heaven-bound children of God."

Dr. Paul Emanuel Larsen,
President Emeritus of the Evangelical Covenant Church

"A MUST READ book for everyone; not only for the believer, either to solidify his assurance or to bless him with that longed for certainty, but also for the unbeliever to warn and produce conviction by the Word. Though well-substantiated by appropriate Scripture verses, *Assured of Heaven* is delightfully interesting because of the expression of personal feelings and experiences. Though authored by a theologian, it is written in a language that is easily read and hopefully understood by one with no background in theology."

Dr. Keith Knopf,
Medical Doctor and Church Leader

"To believe there's a heaven yet have strong doubts about getting there is to suffer a singular kind of torment. Bob Ricker makes a strong, compelling case that believers need not just hope but can *know* with certainty where they will spend eternity. He does so by raising valid, plaguing questions and then sharing biblical truth in ways that speak assurance to both mind and heart. This life is too short and forever is too long not to be *Assured of Heaven.*"

Pamela Heim,
Speaker and Trainer on Leadership and Spiritual Life

"You cannot read ten pages of Dr. Ricker's book without seeing a quintessential pastor's heart for people. This book is replete with astute biblical answers, heartfelt authenticity, and profound wisdom for everyone wrestling with the core issues of life and faith."

Dr. Troy Dobbs, Senior Pastor, Grace Church,
Eden Prairie, Minnesota

"Dr. Robert Ricker addresses one of the critical issues that is important to the stability and confidence of every person who wants to have a strong enduring walk with Christ. His treatment of this subject will bring a level of peace and confidence that every believer needs."

Dr. John Jenkins, Senior Pastor,
First Baptist Church of Glenarden, Landover, Maryland

"Veteran believer/pastor/statesman Bob Ricker, sharing his own Bunyanesque experiences, has written on a critical theological topic addressing disturbing questions in normal Christian growth."

Dr. Jim Lutzweiler,
Archivist/Rare Book Curator, Southeastern Baptist
Theological Seminary, Wake Forest, North Carolina

"For seekers who wonder if there's a basis for assurance of heaven or for believers who struggle with doubts, this book offers a treasure of wisdom. The frequently quoted Scripture passages provide authority, Bob Ricker's transparent description of his personal struggle creates authenticity, and the multiple illustrations provide applications to a wide variety of people and circumstances. On every page Bob's pastor's heart and his love for God and His Word shine through. Reading it was like being on a spiritual retreat."

Dr. Leland Eliason, Pastor, Provost of Bethel Seminary,
and Vice President of Bethel University

"Two great tragedies exist in the Christian Church. One is that many true believers in Jesus Christ lack assurance of salvation and an eternal home in heaven. The other is that some professed believers think they are going to heaven but will never get there unless they realize the errors of their beliefs and come with simple faith in Jesus Christ alone. Bob Ricker writes from both his personal and pastoral experience and explains in great detail the biblical answers to both situations. Read this book and discover how and on what basis you can be sure of heaven."

Rev. Richard Varberg,
Missionary, Church Leader, and Author

The Author's Children Weigh In:

"This book begins with a startling admission by its author: 'Call me "Thomas," the doubting disciple.' In *Assured of Heaven*, Dr. Ricker (or, as I like to call him, 'Dad') confronts everyday crises of faith with clarity, certainty, and honesty. As you read this book, enjoy the stories, the assurances, and the profound wisdom from which I continue to learn every day of my adult life."

Todd Ricker

"Everyone needs this book! Either you've had doubts or you can help someone else who has! If we know something to be true, we must tell others. *Assured of Heaven* makes that task fun and easy to accomplish. The conversational tone in which it is written makes it an enjoyable read. Now you can experience the joy I had growing up listening to Bob Ricker—my dad—tell stories and make biblical truths come to life."

Kristen Wise

Assured of Heaven

Defeating Doubts and Confirming Certainty

Bob Ricker

Foreword by George Verwer

Preface by Marilyn Meberg

ASSURANCE BOOKS

© 2009 by Robert S. Ricker

Published by Assurance Books
P.O. Box 1747, Thousand Oaks, California, 91358
www.assurancebooks.com

First printing, October, 2009

Printed in the United States of America

ISBN 978-0-578-03386-0

With unending love and appreciation I dedicate this book to my mother and dad, Rev. and Mrs. S. D. Ricker, for their unconditional love as well as their biblical modeling and teaching. No child could ask for more than I received from them. They are now in heaven with their Lord and Savior whom they loved with all their hearts. Besides a grateful family, they leave a legacy of the churches they served and non-churched people whom they befriended with the love of Jesus Christ. They remain dear to the hearts of a multitude of people, many of whom they led to the Lord. I miss them.

Contents

Foreword

I have been amazed over the years to discover how many Christians, who seem to really know Christ, do not have full assurance of their salvation. This book could make the difference for them.

I have known Bob for over 40 years and I know he "walks the talk" and for me that is important. Please take a moment to read the Contents page and you will see important chapters you may want to go to right away about something that is on your heart at this time.

I recommend this book for serious Bible study groups because it has great study questions at the end of each chapter. Keep in mind that you don't have to understand and agree with everything you read. Keep going back to the Scriptures. In my own struggles with doubt, I was greatly helped by a Scottish theologian who said that great faith is not in the absence of doubt, but often as we walk our way through it. My prayer is that you will grow stronger in your faith.

George Verwer
Founder of Operation Mobilization

Preface

You are about to read the most important book you will ever encounter. It is brilliant. I say that not because Bob Ricker is one of my favorite persons on the planet or even that I'm honored he happens to be my cousin. The simple truth is this book addresses every issue of the questing and burdened human heart. "Can I lose my salvation? What is the unpardonable sin? Have I committed it? Have I sinned so much God gives up on me? What about my doubts? Why do I have doubts?"

Bob is a well-trained biblical scholar. Like any reputable scholar, he examines the original languages in order to ferret out the exact truth of God's message to His people. As a result, the reader feels confident and can say, "Hey, Bob knows what he's talking about!"

One of my favorite statements Bob writes is "...no verse in Scripture makes another verse untrue... Each verse should be interpreted in the light of the entire Bible. Every verse is true. Every verse has its part in the whole of the message of God as He reveals Himself to us."

Bob makes the verse connections so clear. That then calms the anxious heart in its search for assurance. Assurance is there.

It is God's gift. Bob makes sure we understand that amazing gift so we are better able to receive it.

There is an unusually sweet family connection between Bob and me. His father Sanford and my father Jasper were brothers. It was Sanford who introduced Jesus to my resistant father. Dad was fiercely independent with seemingly unattainable goals. He was determined he needed no one but himself. Sanford persistently told Dad he needed Jesus. Dad persistently said he didn't. When the banks failed in the 1930s, taking every penny of Dad's hard-earned wages, Sanford introduced Matthew 11:28 to my deeply discouraged father. "Come to me all of you who are weary and carry burdens. I will give you rest."

Dad yielded then to the message of Jesus; the one who took his sin as well as his burdens upon Himself. Ultimately, both brothers, from a family of 10 children, entered the ministry and unfailingly preached the truth of God's message of salvation to all who would believe and receive.

Bob comes from a rich heritage. Both Uncle Sanford and Aunt Grace committed all their energies to minister to whomever and wherever God called them. Their three children, Phyllis, Sandy, and Bob, all responded to the same God-call. Each has spent their adult lives sharing who Jesus is and how to know Him personally. I love them, respect them and am so proud to be a Ricker!

Proverbs 23:24 "The father of a righteous person will rejoice greatly; whoever fathers a wise child will have joy in him."

You, cousin Bob, are a "wise child."

Marilyn Meberg
Author and Speaker for Women of Faith

Acknowledgements

Many wonderful people have joined me in various ways in the writing of this book. As many of the professional athletes say on camera after a big win, "It was a team effort." My fear is leaving someone out.

Tim Remington edited this book. I had the privilege of being his pastor at Grace Church in Edina, Minnesota. He is presently in full-time church pastoral ministry (See page vii). Editing is a huge task. With a great spirit, creativity, freshness, and eager to communicate the message of this book, he has been a God-send to me. Julie Saffrin was a big help to him in that process. Coming alongside of us is my younger sister, Sandy Alger who, as a teacher and a first-class student, has given untold hours ensuring that we are consistent with the grammatical standards of the day. She is also very active in her husband's business and in their church, particularly as a keyboard musician.

Some of you have found the book through the superb work of another friend of mine, Dick Lundborg. He has been ahead of the curve in helping Christian causes with both ideas and creative ways to use cutting edge technologies. I am pleased he was willing to use his talents to help get the word out on this book.

In addition to offering great appreciation to the the four I just mentioned, I want to thank all those who gave endorsements. Have you ever thought of what it takes to endorse a book? Reading, pondering, deciding if they should endorse, and then writing what they feel is their proper statement regarding the book. I carefully selected those whom I wanted to present this book to you. I am grateful to each one. I have included their endorsements, with their complete bios available on the website.

I am not blessed with either great computer knowledge nor the intuitive ability to navigate the intricacies of a computer and I get no joy figuring them out. I appreciate Dale and Sharon Morgan who have been generous with their time and skills keeping one or more of my computers running and providing guidance along the way. Sharon also developed two websites: one personal—www.bob-ricker.com, and the publisher's website, www.assurancebooks.com. Working with Sharon was Emmalee Gebo, graphic designer of the Assurance Books website as well as provider of other art work. Her mother, Rose Gebo, wrote copy for the web sites and strategized ways to generate web traffic for the book. Thanks to each of these magnificent Christian people.

Then there are two Parkers for whom I am deeply grateful: father and daughter. Jennifer Parker designed the cover for *Assured of Heaven*. A professional, she is a strong talent and, as all the people mentioned, very nice to work with. Her dad, the very well-known church musician, one of America's finest, Ken Parker, is also one of the most creative people I know. When I was struggling with what to name the project, I turned to him. The first suggestion on his list was the one I used—it was right on target.

Many Christian friends have been of enormous help during the writing of this book. There are too many to name here even though the conversations were often intense, helpful, and stimulating. Many encouraged me by telling me of their need for a book like this.

My great thanks to Rev. George Verwer for writing the Foreword. Being the founder of Operation Mobilization, which has sent out 120,000 missionaries around the globe, he is a busy man. I hesitated even asking him to write the Foreword, but my desire for him to do it outweighed my hesitation. He is one of my heroes. Every time I am with him, I am challenged to do more for God. As I look back over my life, I realize our 40-year friendship has been of no small privilege.

I have deep gratitude to my cousin Marilyn Meberg for writing the Preface. It has been a great joy to see how God has used her to impact millions of women through her books and as one of the speakers for Women of Faith. I didn't want to take advantage of our relationship by asking her to do this, but you can see I did. In the midst of certain conversations, I will ask women if they know my cousin Marilyn Meberg and with excitement they respond, "Oh yes! ... she's your cousin?"

Dee, my cherished wife, has walked with me in this two-year journey of writing. So often there was the closed office door which, of course, she could have opened, but in order to partner in this task, didn't unless necessary. There were times when we could have taken a short or long trip, but the book compelled us. Thanks, Dee, I love and appreciate you.

There are eight other people who have been of immense encouragement in our lives and in our ministry. Our son

Todd and daughter Kristen, who mean more to us than all the world—they are our biggest fans. What a blessing they are! Both have strong marriages—Sandra with Todd and Michael with Kristen. We have great love and respect for all of them. Michael and Kristen have our four wonderful grandchildren: mcKensey, Harrison, Jackson, and Dawson.

And thanks to you, dear Lord, for leading me out of the valley of doubt into the sunshine of certainty. Thank you for what I felt was an urging from You to write this book as a tool in three circumstances: to share our journey to heaven with others, to help Christians who struggle with doubts, and to increase believers' peace and joy in being *Assured of Heaven*.

Bob Ricker

About the Editor

Tim Remington has been in communications work within the Christian community for more than 20 years. He has authored many articles that have been printed in Christian publications, is a playwright, and is working on a novel. *Assured of Heaven* is his third editing project. You can contact him at tim@tcremington.net.

A Terrifying Fear

Have you doubted that you will go to heaven? Does that thought scare you? As a pastor, my life experience of working with people leads me to believe most genuine Christians have doubts—ranging from occasional doubts to obsessive doubts, or somewhere in-between.

As a child, I thought about the length of eternity—no end to it! I didn't want to be in the wrong place. What I read in the Bible about hell kept me awake at night. I wanted to know for sure I was going to heaven but I didn't know how to find out. I went to church, Sunday school, Wednesday night prayer meeting, Bible school, Bible camp, and evangelistic meetings. I memorized Scripture, had daily devotions with my family, and yet couldn't nail down if I was a genuine Christian on my way to heaven.

I was embarrassed to let anyone know about my doubts. This struggle went on for years. I was terrified I would come to the end of life and the fears and doubts would still be there. What if the Lord returned, taking my family to heaven to be with Him, leaving me alone on earth? Irrational fears of being in a fatal car accident or being terminally ill tormented me—I knew there was nothing worse than going to eternal condemnation because my salvation wasn't real. The death rate is 100 percent and I knew someday it would be my turn—not knowing where I would spend eternity was ongoing torture. You may have deep concerns as well. Ecclesiastes 3:11 tells us that God has placed eternity in all human hearts. Many won't admit this and seek to mask it, but the consciousness is there.

I have had about every doubt in the world. Call me "Thomas," the doubting disciple. Having worked through my doubts, I am compelled to write. I have much empathy and sympathy with doubters. I hope that my unpleasant journey of doubts helps you and those with whom you share the biblical truths in this book. This book is a manual for helping people with doubts, helping people who are helping others with doubts, and increasing your peace and joy in being assured of heaven. An additional goal is to explain how you, or someone else, can become a true child of God.

Assured of Heaven will help you deal with doubts and be certain you are going to heaven. I want you to overcome your fears and be confident of your eternal salvation. My hope and my prayer is that this book will help you and those whom you know who struggle with doubt. Don't give up figuring it out! Or worse, don't assume you are going to heaven without understanding what salvation through Christ means.

A recent poll reveals that less than one percent of Americans believe they are going to hell. Are there many or few who are going to heaven? Does everyone end up there? Is there a way to find out? If some are going to heaven and others are not, what makes the difference? You will find out in this book.

Beliefs about Getting to Heaven

✓ Most people believe living a good life is what will get us into heaven even though the Bible says our good works *can't* earn us salvation. It also says those who don't take care of their sin problem (Is anyone without a sin problem?) will not get to heaven. That's scary stuff! Furthermore, the Bible says, "...wide is the gate and broad is the road that leads to destruction, and many enter through it. But small is the gate and narrow the road that leads to life [this includes heaven], and only a few find it" (Matthew 7:13-14).

"I can't imagine a loving God sending anyone to hell," is a common statement. Where does the confidence come from that these seemingly reasonable words are correct? Not in Scripture—somebody just made that statement up! So then, why do we think it is true? If someone says, "My God won't send anyone to hell," they are setting themselves up as the authority.

✓ Some say that if a person has faith they will get to heaven—any kind of faith—just faith. Well, everyone has faith! Everyone lives by faith—we all trust in something or someone. Some trust in what they "think." But is our faith based on truth? Faith in just having faith does not give us assurance that we are going to heaven.

Struggling with doubt is not the most frightening condition—not having prepared for eternity is! Those that haven't prepared are often those who assume everything will turn out fine. After all, they know people who don't live as good a life as they do. They may have the idea that "all roads lead to the same place," but this has no basis in fact, either. Not all roads lead to heaven and sincerity alone is not enough. What good is sincerity if you are on the wrong road? There have been times traveling when I sincerely thought I was on the right road. I was wrong. People will only get to heaven if they are on the right road—meeting the conditions set by God. Wonderful people—some even calling themselves Christians; baptized, confirmed, taken communion, done good works, and members of a church—but they have not met Christ's simple requirement and are on their way to an eternity without Him to a place the Bible calls, "the lake of fire" (Revelation 20:15). Scripture declares, "There is a way that seems right to a man, but in the end it leads to death" (Proverbs 14:12).

Some live by faith in God and His Word, the Bible. Others trust that they have within themselves the right answers. Will your belief survive God's test when you stand before Him who is both judge and jury? I want something or someone greater than myself as my authority on that day. If my confidence is in Jesus Christ and His Word, I can stand on the Day of Judgment with confidence.

I wrote this book to confront the widespread doubts, fears, and misconceptions about salvation amidst the infinitely high stakes of eternity. In the city of my first pastorate, a particular house was scheduled to be demolished. The crew arrived and pushed over the house with a bulldozer. They then scooped it into a truck, cleaned the lot, and left. Their task was finished. The only problem—they had the wrong house! Are you like the bulldozer—headed for the wrong place when this life is over? If you aren't sure, don't be embarrassed. Nearly everyone wonders, including many Christians. I was a wondering Christian during the years of my greatest doubts.

Is Christianity exclusive? Yes, but salvation is available to everyone who wants to come to Christ by faith (John 14:6, Acts 4:12). Jesus, Himself, said there is only one way and part of the good news of the Gospel is that one way is enough! The plan of salvation is marvelously simple yet it is adequate. This will be explored in Chapter 3.

The Bible Is Our Authority

You may ask: "On what basis do you give this spiritual guidance?" The Bible is my source and authority. The Bible is God's inspired Word to man and it gives the answers we need. Some feel the Bible is subject to a wide variety of interpretations and is too difficult to understand. Neither is true. If you read the Bible as you would another book—say a history book—and take it for what it obviously says, you'll understand most of it clearly. Mark Twain said, "It's not the things I don't understand in the Bible that bother me, it's the things I *do* understand!" Granted, there are a few parts of the Bible no one understands completely. The Scriptures themselves say, "The secret things belong to the Lord our God" (Deuteronomy 29:29). However, the subjects of salvation and eternal life are clearly presented and easily understood in the Bible.

In *Assured of Heaven* I want to take you on a journey—my journey of resolving doubts. There is help for you or your friends who are plagued by doubt. After all, the next life lasts a long time—a lot longer than our present life—and no one gets out of this life alive! Resolve this issue. It will change your life. I am glad I went on this journey. I will be even happier if you go with me and allow me to share with you what I have discovered because, right now, I look forward to the next life and an eternal future there. I know how to defeat the doubts that come along and confirm the certainties recorded in Scripture. There is good news for you. You can know without a doubt you are going to heaven. Read carefully and prayerfully.

Summary of the Introduction

This life is a comparatively brief and temporary experience and after it we face eternity in one of two destinations: a place wonderful beyond description or a place terrible beyond description.

My dad, as he was growing older, often said, "It is better on ahead." That is now part of his experience. As good as this life can be, the next one is infinitely better for those who know Christ in a personal way. Heaven is our greatest hope. Everyone thinks about the next life though many won't admit it. The Bible tells us that God has placed eternity in our hearts. It is gracious of Him to do this and it is extremely serious for anyone to ignore it.

Where are you in all of this? Most people have some doubts about their eternal destiny. One of the greatest things to happen in my life was getting rid of my doubts about where I would spend eternity. Perhaps God allowed me to have these doubts and then led me out of them so I can help others. I would be delighted if many could find their way out of doubts and into assurance through this book.

In these matters God has given us His Word, the Bible, to be the authoritative guide. He created us and He has graciously given us a marvelous road map, both for this life and for getting to the next one. Faith in being sincere, or faith in a faith which is not based on truth, is without value. As you read this book you may still have unanswered questions or doubts not dealt with in any of the chapters. You can blog about this and gain further insight. Go to www.assurancebooks.com. Additional help beyond this book is available at this "Command Post for Doubts."

Personal Reflection or Discussion Questions

1. Do you think about the next life? How often?

2. What questions do you have about the next life?

3. Do you think more about it when you go to a funeral?

4. What would you like to know about the next life?

5. Do you think all roads go to heaven? Or, do you think certain roads (plural) lead to heaven? If so, which ones?

6. Are you interested in knowing more about the next life? Why? What do you want to know?

Chapter 1

Consumed with Doubts
John 20:24-25

Doubting and Scared

I wasn't bluffing or looking for sympathy. My heels weren't dug in—I wanted to be *certain* I was going to heaven. Filled with doubts about eternity, I was scared. I had nothing against Jesus, the Bible, or the church but I didn't know where I would spend eternity and I didn't like it that way.

I didn't know what to do. Though my parents were godly, well-educated, and caring, their answers—which worked for others—didn't work for me. I could not have asked for a finer Christian home. Dad was a benchmark father and pastor, my mother an ideal parent and pastor's wife. They were well-loved in every church in which they served, as were Phyllis, the first born, myself, and my younger sister by seventeen years, Sandy. Phyllis was a wonderful Christian role model for me as well as my friend. She taught me what she was learning in school, enabling me to skip right from kindergarten to second grade. Sandy was the very helpful grammarian for this book. I suppose I am biased but it seems as if we had a most desirable home.

Mostly good things were in my life—though one underlying issue was always present—would I go to heaven or hell? Embarrassed to admit my doubts, I kept them to myself until I was in my mid-teens. To one degree or another, they were my companion. On the worst days my doubts were a traumatizing and sad presence. Sometimes I would lie awake at night afraid of going to hell while my family went to heaven. I worried about the "unforgivable sin" mentioned in the Bible (Matthew 12, Mark 3, Luke 12). I read of people who had "been enlightened," "tasted the heavenly gift," and "shared in the Holy Spirit." Hebrews 6 said they even, "tasted the goodness of the word of God," and yet verses 4-6 say: "It is impossible for those...to be brought back to repentance." Hebrews 10:26-27 made me anxious: "If we deliberately keep on sinning after we have received the knowledge of the truth, no sacrifice for sins is left, but only a fearful expectation of judgment and of raging fire that will consume the enemies of God." I knew I had deliberately sinned after I "received the knowledge of the truth" and became a Christian.

Was I doomed? I also knew about predestination at an early age. Was I predestined to be saved? I heard evangelists warn of "sinning away the Day of Grace." What did that mean? Had I done that? I was envious when I saw Christians who seemed free of doubts. Knowing they would have been surprised if they learned about my doubts, I kept them hidden.

To my surprise, after many years in ministry, I have found numerous Christians wrestle with these same doubts—including some evangelical pastors and missionaries. There is even a major Christian denomination that teaches we cannot know we have eternal life until we die. The trouble is—that's too late!

The need for the assurance of heaven is great, but surprisingly little information is available. A book I found while writing this one is *How Can I Be Sure I'm a Christian* by Donald S. Whitney. I commend it.

President Dwight Eisenhower pressed Billy Graham about how people can know they are saved. The often quoted and well-known Christian, John Bunyan, admitted to periods of secret unbelief. This author of *Pilgrim's Progress* even struggled with assurance of salvation. The great "Prince of Preachers" in London for several decades, Charles Haddon Spurgeon, endured dark valleys of doubt and wrote of the experience. If he had doubts, you and I should not be surprised if, at least from time to time, doubts enter our minds. The important thing is to learn how to deal with them. There is a devil the Bible calls our accuser: "...the accuser of our brothers, who accuses them before our God day and night..." (Revelation 12:10). With Satan as our accuser, doubts may cross our minds and try to lodge in our thought processes (Read the context in Revelation 12:7-12).

Be Assured

Let me encourage you at this early part of our journey to assurance of salvation. You may question your devotion to Christ because of your doubts. Yet, if you cared nothing for Christ or faith, would your doubts bother you? They probably would not! Your doubts may indicate you are a person serious about your faith who desires a close relationship with Christ. Doubts can be the other side of the coin of faith.

When Thomas the disciple doubted, the Lord didn't condemn him. After walking into the locked room where the disciples were gathered, the Lord met Thomas at his point of need and gave him the proof he needed to settle his doubts. "My Lord and my God!" Thomas replied with settled faith. His doubts were gone! This is what I longed for and now long for you to have. Jesus then urged Thomas to believe rather than feed on doubt (John 20:27-29). I can relate to Thomas and his need for assurance.

Part of my reason for doubting is that I have an over-inquiring mind. I press issues beyond what is reasonable to most people. As a result I end up with a lot of doubts. During my years of wrestling with doubts, I searched the Scriptures for help. I went into Dad's library in the church and looked for books on assurance of salvation and scanned commentaries looking to see what brilliant biblical scholars had to say about the verses related to my doubts. Though well-written and biblical, they didn't show me how to confront my doubts or handle them.

In my mid-teens I came to the end of the road trying to figure them out on my own. I rallied my courage to drop a bombshell. I found my mother working on the church bulletin. With tears running down my cheeks I said to her, "I don't know if I'm a Christian." Sensing my crushing burden, she put down her work and tenderly and calmly talked to me about what was going on in my heart and mind. My father showed similar compassion and wisdom. I knew they both loved me unconditionally and completely. All of this helped me open the door for both of my parents to think and pray with me and give me advice. Why didn't I do it sooner? I was too ashamed of my doubts.

My public life didn't reflect my doubts. Many times I had given testimony of my faith. President of the local and district youth groups, I often led worship for Dad and participated in the church music program. Seen as a teenager who had it together, I was loved by the congregation which was an extended family to me. I liked being part of a pastor's family.

I believed that salvation was only through Christ and I affirmed that Scripture was inspired. I believed Christ died for me and rose again from the dead. None of the cardinal doctrines of Scripture were a problem to me. I was 90 to 99 percent sure of my salvation. It was the 10 percent or even a one percent chance of being lost that made up the darkest days of my otherwise pleasant growing up years and kept me awake at night. Eternity is real—it lasts a long time! A one percent chance of being lost was not acceptable to me.

"Bobby, why can't you believe?" my parents once asked me in frustration over my continuing doubts. "Your sister doesn't have any problem with doubts—she just believed and was assured of her salvation." "I don't know," was all I could answer. The irony of their question is that I recently learned Phyllis did go through a period of doubting. She tried over and over again to settle her doubts. Like me, she was an outgoing Christian, active in the church, and highly social. She led others to Christ even while she experienced doubts. It astonished me that neither of us knew of the other's struggles with doubt until now, decades later.

As a child I wanted my Sunday School teacher to ask me

if I was sure of my salvation. I wanted to tell him I wasn't sure but I lacked the courage to approach him. He never asked— confident I'm sure—that my faith was secure. With my parents I attended an evangelistic service in a neighboring town at a Christian and Missionary Alliance church. At the invitation I had a strong desire to go forward. Was the Holy Spirit calling me or my own thoughts, rationalizing that if I went forward I would get help with my spiritual dilemma? I don't know. But I was a pastor's son, parents at my side, surrounded by people from our church. Fear of embarrassment constrained me from going forward. That would have taken more humility than I was willing to exercise. In all likelihood my parents and friends would have been delighted that I was serious about my faith (and doubts). Even if my doubts weren't addressed, it would have been good for my soul if I had gone forward, planted my flag, and made a firm decision for Christ. I have advised some doubters to accept Christ again and record the date so they can go look back at the calendar the next time a doubt comes along.

Sometime later I spoke with my dad about that experience of not going forward and still being filled with doubts. He wisely and lovingly offered to give an invitation in the church service the next Sunday for anyone who "wants to take another step with Christ." He did that for me and I responded. Did it help? Not much, though it was another step in my spiritual pilgrimage.

As a very young person, I continued to search the Scriptures to find a water-tight verse or passage to give me full assurance. Though such verses are there, I found reasons to believe they weren't water-tight. I rationalized Scripture and put qualifiers with the words. For example, Romans 10:13 says, "Everyone who calls on the name of the Lord will be saved." I added, "unless you have doubts." Sometimes I tagged a second verse onto the verse that gave the promise, such as with verses that spoke of the unpardonable sin (See Chapter 5). While the Bible is its own best interpreter and while we should ideally bring all Scripture to bear on all Scripture in our interpretation, no verse in Scripture renders another verse untrue. This was a vital and necessary truth for me to grasp in climbing out of my doubts. Let the Scriptures speak for themselves! I believe the larger issue is that when we are tenacious in seeking the Lord with all our heart, He will show us His path.

We Have an Enemy

Satan is clever. He knows if he can keep us from the certainty of our personal salvation we will not live out the fullness of the spiritual experience we actually possess. He loves to take our favorite verses and diminish their impact by convincing us they mean less than God intended. Then we don't glean from them the assurance of our salvation. He twists Scripture or plants doubt by saying, "If you were really a Christian, this would be true of you, or for you." An example is the powerful hope of the church, the return of Christ. If we don't know we will go to heaven when Christ returns, why would we want Him to come back? And yet, the return of Christ is our greatest hope; it is the hope which is adequate for us regardless of what we go through during our time on earth.

Why did I enter this long season of doubt? Perhaps, in part, because when I accepted Christ there was no dramatic change. I'm not sure when I was "born again" because, just to be sure, I accepted Christ at least a thousand times! At family devotions when I was 5 years old, I prayed, "Dear Jesus, come into my heart and make me good so when I am big I can be a preacher like my dad." Was that when I first placed my faith in Christ? Perhaps. I came with my nothingness to receive His everything. I came as a child with a child's faith. I didn't understand justification or sanctification. I just knew I wanted and needed to receive Christ. There was no sudden change in my life that anyone could recognize. I didn't have a drug or alcohol problem, no adultery, or prison time! So, was I saved or lost? I hasten to say that it was a great blessing to be saved "from it" rather than to be saved "out of it." However, as I grew older I saw dramatically changed lives in others who came to know Christ.

My parents led a lot of people to Christ. Their witness included some in our community who were far from the kingdom. I remember one woman who was hardened to the Gospel. Mother and Dad visited her time and time again. One day I saw this stern woman coming to our front porch. It was my mother's birthday. Mother invited her in and they had the privacy of the porch. This woman blurted out, "Do you think God can save a sinner like me?" A little while later I caught a glimpse of the two of them kneeling by the couch on the porch as this woman was transferred from the kingdom of darkness to the kingdom of light. Until my mother passed away, every year she received a birthday card from this lady, including a reminiscence of being born again on my mother's birthday. A new creature in Christ Jesus, this woman's life changed—even her face transformed from hardness to peacefulness. Nothing that dramatic happened to me.

As you read this book and I deal with various doubts, be sure you do not leave any of the chapters that strike some chord of doubt within you until you have worked them through. Deal with any latent doubts that come to mind as you read. You and I don't need to live with doubts. We can know! And the person you are trying to help can know! The next chapter speaks to the issue that we, in fact, can know.

Salvation, and knowing for certain we have it, is the most important subject known to anyone. In Luke 10:20 after the 72 disciples joyfully told the Lord even the demons submitted to them in His name, Jesus said, "However, do not rejoice that the spirits submit to you, but rejoice that your names are written in heaven."

Satan plants doubts. We should not underestimate what a nuisance and power he is for evil. As a deceiver, he has a multitude of demons at his disposal. When he comes with doubts, take a biblical path out of that doubt. He will likely keep coming after us, but there is a pathway in every instance—a way to defeat Satan! First John 4:4 says, "...the one who is in you is greater than the one who is in the world." At the same time, we should not "look for a demon under every bush." Often people blame Satan for things he didn't do. It may have even been something good, sent by God but not recognized by us as good. However, Satan is a problem. "Satan himself masquerades as an angel of light" (2 Corinthians 11:14). What better weapon could he have than to appear as a representative of God and give us doubts as to whether or not we are forgiven? He points his ugly finger at us and puts questions in our minds—why look forward to heaven if we don't know we are going there? He discourages and hinders our witness because we don't have assurance we are saved. This doubt even tarnishes our enthusiasm for financially

supporting God's work because we don't know what our standing is regarding the kingdom of God.

Satan knows a lot about us and he knows a lot about God. He
is an accurate theologian. He knows what is going to happen to
him (Revelation 20:10). Cast out of heaven, he knows a lot about
it and has access to the throne room because he is standing
before God "day and night" accusing us (Revelation 12:10). "Be
self-controlled and alert. Your enemy the devil prowls around
like a roaring lion looking for someone to devour. Resist him,
standing firm in the faith, because you know that your brothers throughout the world are undergoing the same kind of sufferings" (1 Peter 5:8-9). Satan is a vicious enemy and comes in
cunning and powerful ways. Second Corinthians 4:4 calls him,
"The god of this age..." and 1 John 5:19 says, "...the whole world
is under the control of the evil one." Satan has been a nuisance
for a long time.

The Holy Spirit convicts us of sin but Satan points the finger of indictment and accusation at forgiven people. Ironically,
Satan tempts us to commit the sin in the first place and then,
after we are forgiven by God, he comes back and pronounces us
guilty of the sin we committed. Satan may do this over and over
regarding a particular sin.

What a difference between God and Satan! After God forgives our sins He says, "...I will forgive their wickedness and
will remember their sins no more" (Jeremiah 31:34). The process must work something like this: Satan tempts us, we yield,
God forgives us, and Satan comes back to accuse. We go to God
a second time and ask Him to forgive our sin and, because He
remembers our sin no more, He says, "What sin?" How can we
tell the difference between the conviction of the Holy Spirit and

Satan's accusations? The Holy Spirit convicts us with the purpose of bringing us to Christ in repentance and faith in the forgiveness He offers through His shed blood on the cross. On the other hand, Satan nags us after we receive Christ's forgiveness and causes us to doubt our forgiveness. The difference between the Holy Spirit's conviction and Satan's accusations are often difficult to distinguish other than through understanding what the forgiveness of God means and how it takes place. God is always ready to forgive. After we are forgiven, Satan is always ready to accuse.

Winning the Battle of Assurance

In my journey there were things I needed to learn about assurance of salvation and misconceptions I needed to "unlearn." As a youth, a couple of my peers lived on a poor farm. Money was scarce. They had to work hard—too hard, perhaps. Life was stark and meager; yet they seemed to have had an assurance of their relationship with Christ and didn't worry about the things that worried me. I envied them and would have traded my almost ideal life for theirs. My living situation was so much better, but assurance of salvation was infinitely larger to me than any of the things on my long advantage list. I'd have taken the poverty over the anguish of doubt.

Many devout believers agonize over their doubts. They are ashamed to admit their doubts for fear people will think less of them; so they are hesitant to ask for help. I found it hard to go to my parents. And now, with decades of ministry experience, I know that a significant percentage—possibly a majority of genuine believers—have this problem, at least from time to time. Some are willing to ask for help, such as a young woman who came to me in tears and shared her problem. Her desperation was greater than her embarrassment and she brought her husband with her. He listened as she poured out her heart and wept and as she and I discussed her doubts. What a sincere soul she was as she opened up her heart in a desire to be sure of her salvation. How great is our relief when we find help in resolving our doubts.

God graciously uses people who doubt and I have been encouraged that He has been willing to use me. God will use us, as imperfect in our faith as we are. I often think of Mark 9:24: "I do believe; help me overcome my unbelief!" God used both my sister and me in leading people to Christ even when we were at war in our souls over the issue of assurance.

As I moved along in life and ministry, my faith strengthened and my doubts were dealt with in ways I will share with you in this book. Whether you are reading this book to help others or to help yourself, I commend you for studying this issue for whomever it may benefit. It will delight me if this book helps you and others. Succeeding pages will deal with the major reasons for doubt and outline a path to truth in the Scriptures and, with that, our assurance of salvation. We will sing with gusto: "Blessed assurance, Jesus is mine!" and know it is true. Major doubts will be dealt with one at a time and the biblical path to victory over them will be shown.

We will win the battle! Let's do it now—remember, "...the one who is in you is greater than the one who is in the world" (1 John 4:4). I understand the phenomenal impact on a person's life when they are not sure. I mentioned before that a 99 percent assurance was not good enough for me. Is it for you? What if you needed to go to the grocery store and you were told if you went right now there was a one percent chance your home would be invaded, your family killed and, upon your return, you would also be killed. One percent odds would not be acceptable. You would do whatever it took to ensure you and your loved ones were safe and protected. Now compare this extreme hypothetical situation with eternity. If a one percent chance of being killed going to the store is unacceptable, surely a one percent chance of being eternally lost will not work either.

Earlier I mentioned doubts can be the other side of faith. If a person has no faith, why would they have doubts? Can you doubt something you believe does not exist? If doubts are inevitable with many Christians and given that there is a devil who is "the accuser," how can this book carry with integrity its promise of "confirming certainty" of the assurance of heaven? It is a strong title and some believe its promise is impossible. However, the basis for the book's title comes from the Bible itself because it says we *can* know we are going to heaven. "I write these things to you who believe in the name of the Son of God so that you may know that you have eternal life" (1 John 5:13). Much more will be said about this verse in Chapter 2.

The aim of this book is to show you how to work through your doubts with the authority of Scripture so that you come to have 100 percent certainty you are going to heaven. This does not mean Satan will never be back trying his old tricks of sowing doubt. However, God intends that our certainty include not even a one percent doubt because He told us we can "know." What a blessing to me to finally "know" after struggling with so many doubts over a number of years.

If you have not placed your faith in Christ, you should have great concerns. Let's reference Matthew 7:13-14: "Enter through the narrow gate. For wide is the gate and broad is the road that leads to destruction, and many enter through it. But small is the gate and narrow the road that leads to life, and only a few find it." According to these verses, the majority of the world's people are headed for an eternity without Christ. There is only one road leading to heaven and those not on it will miss heaven. Jesus made this clear as he answered Thomas' direct question on how to get to heaven: "Jesus answered, 'I am the way and the truth and the life. No one comes to the Father except through me'" (John 14:6). Chapter 4 deals thoroughly with the one and only way.

The Bible is the basis for our assurance of salvation. In the Bible God reveals Himself to us. It is the Bible where God tells us what we need to know. God, in His own way, let the writers of the Bible know what to write. Also in His own way, God super-intended the process of preserving the Scriptures down through the ages to the extent that we can hold up the Bible and say, "This is the Word of the Lord." Resources to help you study the reliability of the Bible are included elsewhere in this book.

Upon the strength, authority, and clarity of the Bible I can write a book with a title that claims assurance of heaven. We are talking about an enormous issue. Second Peter 1:3-4 gives us this insight: "His divine power has given us…his very great and precious promises, so that through them you may participate in the divine nature and escape the corruption in the world caused by evil desires." One of these "very great and precious prom-ises" is that you can know you are going to heaven (1 John 5:13). This verse, or its reference, will be repeated in this book. Do not minimize this verse—it is the Word of the Lord.

Discussion questions at the end of each chapter will assist you if you are using this book in a group setting. If you are studying alone, let the questions be a means of reflecting upon and internalizing the material.

Summary of Chapter 1

Consumed with Doubts

As uncomfortable as doubts regarding our eternal life can be, they are also an indicator that we care about faith and they suggest we have faith. Otherwise we wouldn't be concerned about our doubts. Going through the struggle of doubts to an assurance of faith is ultimately a positive process. To really doubt and to then really know is significant.

If great biblical students and preachers have wrestled with doubts, others will have them as well. The devil is a real nuisance; but he is real nonetheless. His tactics include making you question your faith. He'll use a variety of ways until he finds one that works well on you. Remember, he is called a liar, deceiver, and an accuser of the brethren.

Don't be discouraged by your doubts. Let them help propel you to a strong faith and assurance. Continue through this book. Talk to a trusted friend or pastor and ask for help. Just don't give up. It is worth the pursuit! Doubt robs us of the joy we would experience if we were certain we were going to heaven. We can know that's our next home, that we are already citizens there, and we will be residents forever.

Do you have trouble distinguishing between the devil's accusation and the Holy Spirit's conviction? If so, reread and think deeply about that part of this chapter.

Another tragedy of doubt is that it dulls our enthusiasm for serving Christ and telling others about His love. Telling others about salvation is far more exciting when I know I, myself, am on my way to heaven.

We live in an age where "tolerance" is the religion of many. Some feel it's cool to follow any religion or no religion at all. It is difficult for some to realize Christianity is an exclusive religion. Jesus made it clear there is only one way of salvation. At the same time—while there is only one way—that one way is adequate for anyone, anywhere, whatever sins they have committed, to be eternally saved and secure in Christ. I cannot imagine being satisfied with anything less than 100 percent assurance of salvation when it relates to where we spend eternity! I remember when I feared I would never have it. But, I do! God bless you in this journey! It can have a happy ending.

Personal Reflection or Discussion Questions

1. Are you willing to admit your doubts to yourself, God, and perhaps a "soul-friend"?

2. What are the good potential sides to doubts?

3. Do you think you are an impossible case? Have you given up? Read 1 John 5:13 again. Do you believe God wants you to "know"?

4. Are you ready to embark on a journey of victory over your doubts regardless of the tenacity it may require?

5. Is a one percent chance of going to heaven acceptable to you? Remember, we're talking about "a forever place."

Chapter 2

Does the Bible Promise Conclusive Assurance of Salvation?

1 John 5:13

2 Peter 1:10

2 Corinthians 13:5

Hebrews 10:22

Building Blocks of Assurance

Does the Bible promise full assurance of salvation? The short answer is "yes." However, a lot more needs to be said. The well-known British preacher, C.H. Spurgeon, said he had only met one or two believers who never experienced doubts of their eternal life.

With the stakes being eternally high, we should pursue the

assurance of eternal life. There are biblical paths for believers to follow when tempted with doubts. If we have paths out of *every* doubt, we have assurance of salvation. This book provides these paths, as provided in the Bible.

My favorite verse on assurance is 1 John 5:13: "I write these things to you who believe in the name of the Son of God so that you may know that you have eternal life." There is nothing unclear about the phrase "that you may know." It is for those who "believe in the name of the Son of God." When the writer uses "name of" he is referring to the whole person. If you "believe in the name of the Son of God" you can "know that you have eternal life." Is the Greek word translated here as "know" synonymous with the way we use the word? Does it mean to really know—to know for sure? The word John used here is not the Greek word translated "perceive," but rather one that means "know with settled and absolute knowledge" (Marvin Vincent, *Word Studies in the New Testament,* Volume 3. William Eerdman Publishers, 1946).

Do we make assurance of eternal life too difficult? I did. How much simpler could it be than, "I write these things to you who believe in the name of the Son of God that you may know that you have eternal life" (1 John 5:13). First John 5:1 says, "Everyone who believes that Jesus is the Christ is born of God." Belief in Christ is the issue. This is clear—simply believe. When the jailer in Philippi asked Paul and Silas how to become a Christian they gave him an answer that probably stunned him with its simplicity: "Believe in the Lord Jesus, and you will be saved" (Acts 16:31). That's it! That's the big issue. That's how we receive salvation. You don't have to do certain things to get ready to believe; just believe in the Lord Jesus and you'll be saved. Believe that when He died on the cross and shed His blood it was to take away your sin and give you eternal life. This is the core of what it means to be a genuine Christian. This was significant to the understanding I needed to be assured of salvation. The next chapter, which explains how to become a Christian in more detail, may be the most important in this book.

In addition to 1 John 5:13, other verses tell us we can "know" we have eternal life. "Therefore, my brothers, be all the more eager to make your calling and election sure" (2 Peter 1:10). How do you do that? Read the Bible and study it with others, go to a church that teaches the Bible, read good books that are recommended by those secure in their faith. Be eager to make sure. Put some time into this. You can have the joy of knowing you have eternal life. There is nothing more important. Assurance of your salvation will give you hope in the midst of trials. Our life in eternity is infinitely long and nothing is more important than knowing it will be a good eternity rather than one of punishment. Heaven is going to be good and hell is going to be bad! Scripture encourages assurance. Hebrews 10:22 says, "let us draw near to God with a sincere heart in full assurance of faith." God considers it important as well. He communicates through Paul: "Examine yourselves to see whether you are in the faith; test yourselves" (2 Corinthians 13:5).

2. Another building block in my assurance was realizing every word of Scripture is true. God so supervised the writing of the Bible that the psalmist said, "...the words of the Lord are flawless, like silver refined in a furnace of clay, purified seven times" (Psalm 12:6). The words of Scripture are closely honed and refined. Here is another: "All Scripture is God-breathed and is useful for teaching, rebuking, correcting and training in

righteousness, so that the man [or woman] of God may be thoroughly equipped for every good work" (2 Timothy 3:16-17). This is so much better than God telling us about heaven and hell and then saying, "I hope you have a way of making sure you are going to heaven." God has told us we can know and that we should pursue this certainty. We can be sure of our salvation.

The biblical paths in this book have had a life-changing impact for me. They and other verses will be helpful to you. In any event, use Scripture—it is the living Word of God. God wrote a perfect book. What other kind of book could a perfect God write? Hebrews 4:12 says Scripture is living, active, sharp, and penetrating. It is your defense against Satan. Accepting Scripture's truth about assurance is easier for some than others. While there is that isolated person who is fortunate to have never struggled with this issue, some like me go through a long, hard, though valuable, process. This has caused me to delight even more in now being sure; and my joy has increased as I have come out on the assured side of my struggle.

Taking a wider look at Scripture, nowhere does it say, "and possibly you will receive salvation." Whether in the verses quoted above or others like John 3:16, 1:12, 6:37; Romans 10:13; Revelation 3:20, 22:17, doubt is never associated with salvation. If you meet the conditions, God *will* give you eternal life. In terms of salvation, I mean a full and complete assurance. As this life is temporary and the next life eternal, it is reasonable for you and me to fervently desire certainty. It is unreasonable not to go to any lengths to obtain assurance of salvation. When we step out of this life into eternity, it is extremely important to know we are stepping into God's presence rather than into eternal separation from God.

Four Things to Know about Satan

Scripture tells us four things about Satan that associates him with our doubts. Satan will come back at you until he sees it does no good—you need a biblical path out of your doubts.

1. **He is a liar.** "When he [Satan] lies, he speaks his native language, for he is a liar and the father of lies" (John 8:44). It shouldn't surprise you that he tries to take away our joy of eternal life by telling us we haven't been forgiven; that we don't have eternal life. Satan is smart. He knows how much our salvation means to us. His best strategy to keep us from enjoying our salvation and looking forward to eternity is to cause us to question whether or not we are children of God.

2. **He is a deceiver.** According to Revelation 20:3, 8, and 10, he is subtle. He even comes as an "angel of light" (2 Corinthians 11:14). Satan makes himself look good but he is the devil. Instead of a magnificent angel, he is the master of darkness.

3. **He is an accuser of Christians.** "...the accuser of our brothers, who accuses them before our God day and night..." (Revelation 12:10). God the Holy Spirit convicts with the goal of bringing us to repentance. Satan annoyingly accuses, shames, and condemns, making our hope of eternity seem uncertain. There is a difference. The Holy Spirit convicts us of sin for our own good to lead us to repent, believe, and bring us into a close relationship with Christ and changes our outlook so that we look forward to eternity.

4. **He is your enemy who wants to devour you.** Scripture tells us his *modus operandi*: "Your enemy the devil prowls around like a roaring lion looking for someone to devour" (1 Peter 5:8). This "devouring" can range from spiritual defeat and doubt, to Nero's persecution of Christians in the Roman Coliseum, to the greatest persecution of Christians of all time which is going on today. The *Voice of the Martyrs'* newsletter reports more than 400 Christians die every day for their faith.

Use this book to help you conquer doubts and find assurance. Underline the Scripture verses to claim when Satan attacks. He will bring doubts but you can answer them with biblical truth and retain your assurance of eternal salvation. The future can be bright according to James 4:7 which tells us when we resist the devil, he will flee from us. Establish a resistance pattern and it will work for you. James 4:8 states a magnificent alternative: "Come near to God and he will come near to you."

Don't let Satan take away your joy or dim your hope of eternity with Christ. He wants to do that because he knows what his doom is (Revelation 20:10). While he is in the Lake of Fire, we will enjoy the presence of Jesus as well as the redeemed through the ages, including loved ones who know the Lord. We will enjoy the new heaven and the new earth in a society that is sinless and perfect. We will ultimately be in the new heaven and new earth—which we typically refer to as "heaven."

While you may be one of those fortunate people who never doubted your salvation, I am concerned about people who blindly assume they will go to heaven. They cite reasons such as: their good outweighs their bad, they have been baptized, confirmed, taken communion, or are members of a church. None of these will take you to heaven. Not all roads lead to the same place. There is only one way to heaven according to John 14:6 and Acts 4:12, among other verses. If you want to spend eternity in heaven, be sure you look seriously at the next chapter. People who fool themselves with a false assurance should heed the warnings in Matthew 7:22-23, Luke 18:11-14, and 2 Corinthians 10:12.

My hope and prayer is that at some moment in this chapter or in this book, your point of doubt becomes a pathway out of the doubt into certainty, as the Bible promises. If your point of doubt hasn't been covered in this chapter, read on as another chapter likely will. Another option is to get more help from our website at www.assurancebooks.com.

Facts That Confirm Our Belief

Having studied the Scriptures for more than five decades, and with the personal confirmation of God, the Holy Spirit within me, I have no doubt but that these Scriptures are the Word of God. I have read well-written books and studied under brilliant scholars, discovering from them reasons for believing the Bible is the Word of God and is reliable for what we believe and as a guide for life. While a believer's final confirmation comes from the Holy Spirit who indwells them (1 Corinthians 6:19), there are facts that confirm and substantiate our belief and convictions.

We Can Trust the Scriptures

Their Unity: The Scriptures were written over a period of 1200-1400 years in different countries, obviously by people who didn't know each other. The one seamless, concurring, and compatible theme is the redemptive plan of God in Jesus Christ and it is the thread that runs through each of the 66 books of the Bible. This unity is further seen in the lack of contradictions. Try writing a book on religion using many different authors from different countries, over a period of more than a millennium, and see if you can arrive at the incredible cohesiveness of the Bible.

Life Change: Another reason we know the Scriptures are true is the life change we see in believers: "Therefore, if anyone is in Christ, he is a new creation; the old has gone, the new has come" (2 Corinthians 5:17). Scripture claims that when a person becomes a Christian, he is "born again" (John 3:3). Just as our physical birth makes us a person of flesh, being "born again" makes us a person of the Spirit (John 3:6). This confirms the validity of Scripture.

Fulfilled Prophecy: There is a great amount of prophecy in the Scriptures. Only God could probe the future with clear, definite prophecies that are coming true just as they were predicted. People unwisely follow psychics such as Jeane Dixon who stated her predictions came true only 60 percent of the time. Biblical prophecies have a 100 percent track record—without stretching the interpretations of prophecies. They have come true literally and in the stated sequence of Scripture. Prophecies about the future will do the same. Seven hundred years before the birth of Christ, the Old Testament said He would be born in Bethlehem.

That's remarkable considering His mother and stepfather lived in Nazareth. Jesus' violent death was also predicted around 700 years before He died, despite the fact that crucifixion was not yet practiced. Just one example of a prophecy that came true, a favorite of mine, is the coming of Christ. Josh McDowell points out in *More Than a Carpenter* (Tyndale House, 2004) that the Old Testament was written before Christ's birth and yet it has more than 300 references to His coming. Actually there are 60 major prophecies of the coming of Christ and 270 ramifications of His coming. If a person takes just eight of these 60 prophecies and applies the science of probability, McDowell says that we will find "the chance that any man might have lived, down to the present time and fulfilled all eight is 1 in 100 quadrillion (one followed by 17 zeros)." The book helps us comprehend this probability by saying it is as if we were blindfolded and picked a marked silver dollar randomly out of a quantity of unmarked silver dollars sufficient to cover the state of Texas to a depth of two feet. The probability that, traveling to anywhere in the state and choosing only one silver dollar, you would choose the marked silver dollar is the same probability of just eight of the prophecies of Christ coming true in any one person. The reasonable conclusion is these prophecies were given by inspiration of God because all 60 major prophecies and 270 ramifications of His coming were all fulfilled in Christ.

Test of Time: Scripture has stood the test of time. Its critics are legion but the Bible is more prominent now than when the last of it was written about 2,000 years ago. Some of it was written more than 3,000 years ago. Many have sought to disprove it—none have succeeded. The Bible stands. It is the anvil that wears the hammer out. Further, we have very old manuscripts of the Scripture, including the Dead Sea Scrolls, which verify that the Scriptures as we have them are the Word of God. God not only inspired people to write them, but He also superintended the process of getting them to us more than two millenniums after Christ's birth and more than three millenniums after some of the people of the Old Testament lived.

There is so much more to be said about the reliability of Scripture. I refer you to books by Lee Strobel and Josh McDowell for far reaching proofs of Christ's birth, life, death, resurrection, and His future return to earth to receive Christians to join Him for eternity.

Witness of General Revelation

Then there is the witness of natural or general revelation. Psalm 19 and Romans 1 speak of this. Psalm 19 says,

> The heavens declare the glory of God; the skies proclaim the work of his hands. Day after day they pour forth speech; night after night they display knowledge. There is no speech or language where their voice is not heard. Their voice goes out into all the earth, their words to the ends of the world (verses 1-4a).

How can one look at the universe and think it "just happened." When does common sense come into play and people realize that the intricate design of the universe demands a designer?

What if I said to you, "Look at my watch. See the lovely gold on the encasement and the black dial; it keeps almost perfect time. My wife, Dee, just found it one day. No one made it; it just happened. Apparently some sand melted and became glass and it was just the right size for the crystal. Then the adjustable band just happened, too. Inside there are a lot of little parts that work together and the watch tells me what time it is; it just happened all on its own. And, furthermore, it didn't just happen one time. The place where it came from had a hundred of them. Think of that. It's amazing."

You would call me a fool. And yet, many with advanced degrees and educated at our nation's finest schools believe that there was a big bang and the whole universe just happened over many years. No one made it. No one orchestrated the parts of it. It just happened. No one would believe my watch story yet a multitude believe the origin of the universe story. It takes more faith to believe there isn't a designer than to believe there is one. However, even with all the evidence, the Bible itself does not try to prove there is a God. It simply says, "In the beginning God" (Genesis 1:1).

Natural or general revelation is also referenced in Romans 1:18-20:

> The wrath of God is being revealed from heaven against all the godlessness and wickedness of men who suppress the truth by their wickedness, since what may be known about God is plain to them, because God has made it plain to them. For since the creation of the world God's invisible qualities—his eternal power and divine nature—have been clearly seen, being understood from what has been made, so that men are without excuse.

Romans 1 and Psalm 19 indicate all people have a consciousness of God. All unbelievers realize there is something they have
not yet found. Because of this natural revelation available to all
people, God holds them "without excuse" (Romans 1:20).

Jay Kessler, former president of Taylor University in Indi-
ana, spoke at the Chicago-area church Dee and I attended. He
mentioned that a larger percentage of people claim to believe
in God today than did so at the time of our Founding Fathers.
There were more atheists then than now. A poll taken about 10
years ago indicated that about 84 percent of Americans believe
in demons, a higher percentage than you would get anywhere
else on the face of the earth, other than perhaps Thailand.

Consider the immensity of the universe. At the point in the
Milky Way galaxy where our planet is located, earth is moving
at about 490,000 miles per hour, about 136 miles per second. It
takes 200 million years to make one rotation. At the speed of
light, it takes 20,000 years to cross our galaxy and 100,000 light
years to travel its length. Two hundred billion stars fill the Milky
Way—including one named Antares into which you could put
our sun, our moon, and our solar system out to the orbit of
Mars. As massive as our galaxy is, it has a billion distant neigh-
bors. Astronomers say that the number of stars in the universe
equals the number of the grains of sand on all the beaches of all
the shores in all of the earth. One expert tried to communicate
the vastness of space by representing the sun as the dot on the
"i" on a typewriter. The nearest star would be a dot 10 miles
away. Other stars, up to the size of a dime, would be hundreds
of thousands of miles distant.

To explore further evidence to support your faith in the
Scriptures, the following can be of help:

1. *More Than a Carpenter* by Josh McDowell which, though short, is an interesting book. There is a chapter entitled "Are the Biblical Records Reliable?" He cites his references and provides additional ones for further study. McDowell's other books along these lines are *Evidence That Demands a Verdict*, Volumes 1 and 2.

2. Read *Who Moved the Stone?* by Frank Morison, a man who set out to disprove the resurrection of Christ and in the course of his study became a believer in Christ's resurrection.

3. Similarly, Lee Strobel was an investigative reporter who explored Christianity after his wife's conversion. He sought to find information to discredit her faith decision but ended up making a decision for Christ himself. He has applied his journalistic skills to a number of helpful resources including books such as *The Case for Faith*, *The Case for Christ*, and *The Case for a Creator*. Books, DVDs, and online resources are available at his website: www.leestrobel.com.

4. Major systematic theology works provide vast amounts of information. Read through the Contents or the Index to find specific topics. There are many excellent systematic theology books including those by Millard Erickson, Wayne Grudem, and Augustus Strong. Do a word search on the internet on these names and obtain further information on their systematic theology books. I have found them all beneficial.

5. Perhaps the easiest and briefest book on making a case for Christianity is the one by Paul Little, *Know Why You Believe*,

and the companion book, *Know What You Believe.*

Assurances in *Assured of Heaven* can lead most who have doubts to a turn-around experience in their faith. Others may use this book as a first step to climbing out of the abyss of doubt about their salvation and eternity.

This book is not a "bag of tricks" from which you can pull out assurance of your salvation. God has to be involved in this and He wants to be. He will illuminate the Scriptures as you read, study, and meditate upon its truths, "…faith comes from hearing the message, and the message is heard through the word of Christ" (Romans 10:17).

The Hindrance of Holiness

Another obstacle to a person coming to assurance in one's faith is personal holiness. Though a view commonly held, we don't earn heaven through living good lives, but holiness can figure into assurance. A person can block the work of the Holy Spirit in their lives by living a life of sin. The psalmist (66:18) said, "If I had cherished sin in my heart, the Lord would not have listened." While we want to diligently study what the Bible says about assurance of salvation, we must realize that holy living helps to keep the channels clear for God to speak to us. Having said that, God can speak to any person in any condition.

I "had it good" and I still had doubts. I was never successful at denying them, though I tried. May the truths in this book help set you free to face and deal with your doubts. Reflect on these questions and/or discuss them in a group Bible study.

Summary of Chapter 2

Does the Bible Promise Conclusive Assurance of Salvation?

This is important! The primary focus of this book is having 100 percent assurance of salvation. Those who have found complete assurance must remain vigilant as Satan will come back and try to plague them again with doubts. However, your certainty remains because you have a biblical path back to assurance.

If the Scriptures did not promise complete assurance, I would not bother writing this book. However, they do promise complete assurance. Complete assurance is implied over and over again and is clearly stated in 1 John 5:13.

Why then do genuine Christians have doubts? There is a devil whom the Bible calls a liar and deceiver. He is our accuser. He wants to devour us; but the Bible tells us his day is coming! In the meantime he will do all the damage he can by keeping Christians from assurance of salvation. This clouds their joy, anticipation of Christ's return, and effectiveness for Christ. Some Christians have doubts because of how they are wired. My inquiring mind worked against me—leading me to press the issue of assurance unreasonably—but it was where I had to go to be sure.

The many assurances that the Bible is true (I have mentioned some in this book but there are others) give us a place to stand on solid ground as we make our journey to heaven. Be tenacious in this pursuit of assurance. You can get there! God has promised it to you. It is worth any amount of effort. It took me many years, much prayer, and a great deal of study. Read the

Bible. Take a serious look, especially at the verses suggested in this book.

Personal Reflection or Discussion Questions

1. Doubts are common even though people are sometimes embarrassed to talk about them. They feel it demonstrates they are not serious followers of Christ, whereas the opposite is more likely to be true. How does this compare with your perspective on doubts?

2. Satan is called the accuser (Revelation 12:10). He causes some of the doubts. And, some people have more inquiring minds than others. They have a hard time believing something until they have thoroughly checked it out. How can you ensure that your mind is an ally in your assurance journey?

3. First John 5:11, 13; John 6:37b; Romans 10:13; John 1:12-13, 20:31; Hebrews 6:11, 10:22 all relate to the reasonableness of attaining assurance of salvation. Think through how each of these verses relates to your assurance of salvation.

4. Can you add to the reasons given above as to why you believe the Bible to be the Word of God?

Chapter 3

What If You Only Think You Are Going to Heaven?

Matthew 7:13-14

Let's put two things together. Early in the book I mentioned that one out of every 100 Americans believes he or she is going to hell. Place this opinion beside Jesus' statement: "...wide is the gate and broad is the road that leads to destruction, and many enter through it. But small is the gate and narrow the road that leads to life, and only a few find it" (Matthew 7:13-14).

"Only a few find it." This fact has propelled my life and ministry. As unpleasant as a believer may find his or her doubts about salvation, it is infinitely more serious to have an assurance of eternal salvation not based upon truth.

Let's paint a picture. You are watching television. A famous person dies. You and those who knew this person first-hand believe he lived a wicked life. Yet on television the talk is about that person being "up there, in a better place looking down on us." Dee and I had an older handyman. One day, in gratitude for his own good health, he told us, "Yes, I have a number of my golfing buddies up there wishing they could be down here playing golf with me" (They must have really liked golf!). Our hearts find it easy to assume those we care about are in heaven, but to get there all must follow the road the Bible identifies—faith in Christ.

An Assurance Check-up

There are many false assurances of salvation. Maybe you hold on to false assurances and maybe you don't. Maybe you have friends who do. An "assurance check-up" can be helpful. It can affirm or maybe point out a need for you to take a new step toward a relationship with God through Jesus Christ. Presumably you are a good person. Perhaps the most "serious" sins have not been part of your life. An enormous question still remains—what does it take to secure a ticket to heaven?

A divine indictment is upon the human race. We are all sinners at birth (often referred to as "original sin"—read Romans 5) and sinners by practice. Therefore, something has to be done about our sinful condition if we are to enter heaven. Why? Because, heaven has no sin within its boundaries. In the closing book of the Bible it says, "Nothing impure will ever enter it, nor will anyone who does what is shameful or deceitful, but only those whose names are written in the Lamb's book of life"

(Revelation 21:27). This is why it is critical to ask—what have *you* done about your sin?

Good Works

We have all done good works. Many in the world believe those good works will earn them entrance into heaven—as if God uses some sort of divine scales of justice. This prevailing opinion believes if your good deeds outweigh the bad deeds and tip the scale in the good direction, God will grant you salvation. The Bible clearly says we can't earn our way to heaven through good works. "For it is by grace you have been saved, through faith—and this not from yourselves, it is the gift of God—not by works, so that no one can boast" (Ephesians 2:8-9). Note: "not by works." In Titus 3:5 it says, "he saved us, not because of righteous things we had done..."

To those of us who have placed our faith in Christ, good works will be part of our lives, an outflow of our salvation, not the cause of it. Scripture says, "...we are God's workmanship, created in Christ Jesus to do good works, which God prepared in advance for us to do" (Ephesians 2:10). In the book of James it says when we have a genuine faith in Christ, good works will be a result (James 2:14-26).

Here's a fictional, illustrative story of Christ's role in our eternal salvation in heaven: Daniel Curry, a mighty man of God, dreamed that he had ascended to heaven and knocked on the gate. He was told, if he wished, he could appear before the judgment throne and answer for himself. He was carried rapidly away until he came into the presence of a brilliant, shining light. It was a million times brighter than anything he had ever seen on earth and its brightness blinded him. Out of the midst a voice said, "Daniel Curry, have you always been good?" He had to answer, "No." "Have you always been pure?" Again his answer was, "No." "Have you always been charitable in your opinion of others?" "I cannot say that I have been." "Have you always been fair and just in your dealings with others?" "No, I haven't been." Daniel thought the end would come any second, but instead he heard a voice of unspeakable sweetness. He turned toward the sound to see Jesus standing by his side, His face sweeter than any face Daniel had ever seen. "Father, all this man's sin, all his mistakes, every evil action, word, and thought; all of his short-comings, put them all down against me—I have paid for them all. I have made him worthy of heaven."

✓   Most, if not all, religions other than Christianity are "works" religions that believe if you are good enough you will be fine in the next life. But if that were the case, Jesus "died for nothing" as Paul reminds us in Galatians 2:21. Both Proverbs 14:12 and Proverbs 16:25 say, "There is a way that seems right to a man, but in the end it leads to death." At the very least these verses warn us of a colossal danger—the danger of thinking we are on a path to heaven but finding out too late we are on a path to a lost eternity. Through faith in Christ, our inheritance in heaven is made possible by the death of Jesus on the cross.

In my first pastorate I met a man who was the top spiritual leader of a denomination in a highly populated valley in south-ern California. We knew we had major differences in theology and in the course of a conversation we decided to spend half of a day trying to convert each other! We believed it would be a clar-ifying time as well as an opportunity to build our relationship.

At the end of the day, just before we concluded our dialogue, I asked him, "How are you going to get to heaven?" He said, "By good works." I said, "You told me you believe the Bible is God's Word and, therefore, true. Ephesians 2:8-9 says, "For it is by grace you have been saved, through faith—and this not from yourselves, it is the gift of God—not by works, so that no one can boast." So the Bible says it is *not* by good works. Consequently salvation cannot be by good works." His response was, "Well, you just know your Bible better than I do." I replied that regardless, I had only shared with him what the Bible says—not what I came up with on my own or from my church's belief. We ended the conversation on a friendly note, but he insisted that salvation is by works. As the top leader over many churches in a large population center, this was terribly serious. This unbiblical belief is the teaching of his denomination, which is growing throughout the world.

Scripture tells us people generally have a good opinion of themselves. They may, in fact, have many admirable qualities. As they compare themselves with others, they decide they aren't "that bad" so they must be "good enough." Second Corinthians 10:12 speaks of this when it says, "We do not dare to classify or compare ourselves with some who commend themselves. When they measure themselves by themselves and compare themselves with themselves, they are not wise."

To have an all-embracing look at ourselves, we need to look at verses in the Bible such as:

Proverbs 16:2, "All a man's ways seem innocent to him, but motives are weighed by the Lord."

Proverbs 20:6, "Many a man claims to have unfailing love, but a faithful man who can find?"

Proverbs 21:2, "All a man's ways seem right to him, but the Lord weighs the heart."

Proverbs 26:12, "Do you see a man wise in his own eyes? There is more hope for a fool than for him."

Proverbs 28:26, "He who trusts in himself is a fool, but he who walks in wisdom is kept safe."

This plea of looking at ourselves objectively is also encouraged in Isaiah 53:6: "We all, like sheep, have gone astray, each of us has turned to his own way; and the Lord has laid on him the iniquity of us all." Then in the greatest of all theological books, Romans 3:23, "…all have sinned and fall short of the glory of God." As a ministerial colleague said as he held high the Scriptures, "This is the Word of the Lord."

All Roads Lead to Heaven

Another "way that seems right to a man" is the error of thinking all roads lead to the same place and none of them have any specific requirements. Some think a loving God would not condemn anyone to a Christ-less eternity. Tolerance is the religion of many. Your way is "cool" and my way is "cool" and we can follow our own road to heaven. However, God says it isn't that way. He says Christ is the only way of salvation. In fact, the common thread running through all Scripture is that a sinful human being can have his or her sins taken away and be given a home in heaven through Christ, and only through Christ. In John 14:6 Jesus said, "I am the way and the truth and the life. No one comes to the Father except through me." Note the definite article "the" is used. In Acts 4:12 it says, "Salvation is found in no one else, for there is no other name under heaven given to men by which we must be saved."

If You Are Sincere

Another deception from Satan is making a person think sincerity is the defining issue or criteria for gaining eternal life. God loves sincerity but it must be linked with truth. I have heard some say sincerity is all that matters, claiming God will honor your belief, no matter what it is "as long as you are sincere." What if you are sincerely wrong? I was the former president of our denomination and the new president of our school, Bethel University, in St. Paul, Minnesota, was speaking. During his speech, without any warning, my chair collapsed—I was flat on the floor! All eyes turned to me and he stopped speaking. I stood up in total silence. "Mr. President," I said, "I recommend you add a line item in the budget for chairs!" I sat in the chair because I sincerely believed it would hold me. I was sincere, but being sincerely wrong put me flat on the floor.

Being a Christian means you have a personal relationship with Christ. It begins by inviting Christ into your life, coming to Him just as you are, and asking Him to be your Savior and Lord. We place our trust in Him to take away our sins and give us eternal life. Being a Christian does not mean we will never sin again, but it does mean our intention and practice is to live a life of following Christ as we are in relationship with Him. When we sin, we go to Christ and confess. We should confess as often as we are aware we have sinned. As in any relationship, it is good to keep short accounts.

Sincerity is a virtue. In fact, it is essential when one comes to Christ. However, sincerity alone does not replace truth as God defines it. You may be concerned, or are at least curious, about the truth of who will end up in heaven and who will not. Or perhaps you want to help others settle their doubts of assurance. How can one not be concerned about the next life when it is eternal? Revelation 20:15 states, "If anyone's name was not found written in the book of life, he was thrown into the lake of fire." Is there anything even close to the seriousness of this scriptural fact? Do you know people who need to know this truth?

In this fleeting life, we are wise to be careful we are not deceiving ourselves by resting in something we have thought was true but, according to the Bible, is not true. We risk an eternity absent from God and His people, but present with Satan and his people. This is worth self-examination and seeking out the truth.

There Is Good News

We are sinners by birth and choice and cannot save ourselves. However, there is good news and hope for our sin problem. The "Gospel" means "good news" and it brings hope in abundance as we learn Christ died on the cross as our substitute to pay for our sins. He paid the debt of our sins we should have paid but did not have the ability to pay. When we make the decision to accept Christ into our lives to take our sin away and to be our Lord and Master, He removes our sin and guilt, and gives us eternal life. This is good news—this is the best news!

With delight I remember an illustration from my college days at Bethel University. I was a junior studying under the beloved, godly, and brilliant professor, Dr. Bob Smith. The course was "Patterns of Christian Thought." He illustrated humankind's sin dilemma by giving an illustration of a professor and student during an exam. The student had failed to study and the professor knew it. The student looked at the test knowing he could not get a passing grade. The professor saw him struggling and said, "I know you have a problem with this. Go sit at my desk and I will sit at your desk and take the exam for you. I wrote this exam and I know all the answers." If this were to happen, the student would exclaim, "That's good news!"

What Jesus did for us on the cross is good news, in fact, the greatest news for humanity around the world and for all generations. Coming to Christ for salvation begins a new life. As we mature in Christ, we grow in holiness from the sinful life we once lived, and perhaps even cherished. As a result our life changes. An important word in all this, and frequently found in Scripture, is "repentance" which means to change our mind, our values, and turn from our sinful lifestyle. This is both an Old and New Testament theme. King David's repentance is beautifully recorded in Psalm 51: "I know my transgressions, and my sin is always before me. Against you, you only, have I sinned and done what is evil in your sight, so that you are proved right when you speak and justified when you judge." John the Baptist

called the Jews to repentance as, "He went into all the country around the Jordan, preaching a baptism of repentance for
the forgiveness of sins" (Luke 3:3). We live as new creations as
2 Corinthians 5:17 specifies. Jesus also called for repentance:
"...repentance and forgiveness of sins will be preached in his
name to all nations" (Luke 24:47). Following the death, resurrection, and ascension of Jesus, His 12 disciples took up the call
as did Peter at Pentecost. Paul took this message of repentance
to the Gentiles.

What could be more serious than coming to the end of life,
standing before God at Judgment Day and, to your surprise, discovering you are not one of those getting into heaven? During
your lifetime you thought you were all right with God and never
questioned where you would spend eternity. I can't imagine the
horror of coming to the end of life and not knowing if I am a
Christian or not. Voltaire, the well known atheist, died shouting,
"No, no, no." Apparently he had seen something just before he
died. I'd rather be like a saintly woman whose bedside I was by as
she lay dying. She said to me, "Do you see the angels?" I didn't.
"They're right over there," she said as she pointed to the corner
of the room near the ceiling. Though she had a glimpse of something, I did not. However, I have no trouble believing her "near
heavenly" experience. Several times I have heard of such things.
I read recently of when Augustus Toplady, writer of "Rock of
Ages," was in his final moments of life and he said, "No mortal
can live having seen the glories which God has manifested to
my soul" (E. Michael and Sharon Rusten, *The One Year Book of
Christian History*. Tyndale House Publishers, Inc., 2003).

We Need to Make a Decision

I will never forget a phone call when I was in my mid-teens. My dad's church was in the midst of an evangelistic crusade. We returned home from that evening's service and were about ready to go to bed. The phone rang and it was Jim (not his real name), one of the most likeable people in the church. He was always there, often the first to greet you as you entered the sanctuary. Jim had a big smile, a lovely wife, and a big-time job. He was someone Dad had repeatedly asked to consider being a deacon. He always politely declined.

Tonight was different. Jim wanted Dad and the evangelist to come to his home right away. They sat down in his living room as Jim surprised them by saying, "I'm not a Christian. I know I've pretended to be one, acted like one, but all along I've known I wasn't a true believer—I never accepted Christ as my Savior." He knew the main issue— "...to all who did receive him, to those who believed in his name, he gave the right to become children of God" (John 1:12). After sharing his story that night, he invited Christ to be his Savior and Lord.

Have you received Christ as Savior and Lord? Many believe they are Christians, have lived a good life, but haven't made a decision for Christ. Could it be that you think you are ready for eternal life but aren't? Satan is a liar and encourages false hope. He does not want people coming to Christ. This chapter presented some of the primary things that people depend upon to get to heaven. There are other things as well—things that are good in and of themselves but not able to take us to heaven: church membership, baptism, confirmation classes, benevolent acts, financial generosity. Even "going forward" at an evangelistic rally or church service, if there is not true repentance, will not earn us heaven nor will being part of a family of long-time Christians or a self-help change in our life. As helpful and meritorious as these things can be, they cannot remove our sin.

As sin is the most serious dilemma of human beings, the Gospel is the best news ever to come to us. The good news is summarized in the most familiar verse in all of Scripture, John 3:16: "For God so loved the world that he gave his one and only Son, that whoever believes in him shall not perish but have eternal life." That's the wonder and wonderfulness of the cross of Christ. My goal in writing this book is that you, or someone you know, can take advantage of the Gospel and be certain that heaven is your final destination.

Born of the Spirit

Have you begun your relationship with Christ? Have you been, in the words of John 3:3, "born again"? Jesus said in John 3:6-7, "Flesh gives birth to flesh, but the Spirit gives birth to spirit. You should not be surprised at my saying, 'You must be born again.' "

When our son and daughter were born—when flesh gave birth to flesh—it was a near overwhelming experience for Dee and me. Now we are grandparents. We were both at the hospital when our youngest grandchild was born. What a work of Divine providence! How can it be that a man and woman can be God's agents of bringing forth a new life? Who fully understands that "flesh gives birth to flesh"? As we watch that wonderful little guy grow up, play baseball, football, and basketball, go to church and school, and become such an important person to so many of us, the mystery of life continues to unfold. We rejoice that "flesh gives birth to flesh."

Even more miraculous is our spiritual birth when "the Spirit gives birth to spirit." This same grandchild accepted Christ and the Spirit gave birth to spirit. What a great moment it was when this same little person was "born again." Our daughter noticed he was crying in bed one night. She went into his bedroom to see what was wrong. He was anxious about something and God entered into their conversation as it progressed to her asking her little boy if he wanted to accept Christ as his Savior. He said he did. He was ready. She asked if he would like his dad to come to the room and he nodded "yes." So there, on what became holy ground, our grandson placed his faith in Christ with his dad and mom lovingly standing by and rejoicing. All were crying and then the boy's anxiety turned to peace and he fell asleep as a new creation in Christ (2 Corinthians 5:17). He was now born of the Spirit. He had been "born again" (John 3:7).

We were born of the flesh through the agency of our mother and father. We are born of the Spirit through the agency of the Spirit of God. This is when we enter the family of God. John 1:12 states, "…to all who received him, to those who believed in his name, he gave the right to become children of God." Ensuring that we have a place in heaven involves a decision on our part. Emphasizing this fact in his ministry, for decades Billy Graham's broadcast was appropriately called "The Hour of Decision."

The Cost of Sin

Let's look further. I would rather risk redundancy than not be crystal clear. Ecclesiastes 7:20 says, "There is not a righteous man on earth who does what is right and never sins." Romans 3:10-12 makes a clear statement on humanity's condition without Christ: "There is no one righteous, not even one; there is no one who understands, no one who seeks God. All have turned away, they have together become worthless; there is no one who does good, not even one." Later in Romans 6:23 it adds to our understanding by saying, "For the wages of sin is death, but the gift of God is eternal life in Christ Jesus our Lord." Further insight into the universality of our sin problem can be found in 1 Kings 8:46; Romans 3:9-23, 7:18; and 1 John 1:8-10. The Bible says we are all sinners. Even those we recognize to be good people are sinners. Earlier in this chapter I mentioned we are sinners two ways—by birth and by choice. We were born with original sin. When Adam and Eve (whom God had made the federal head of the human race) sinned in the Garden of Eden, the entire human race fell. Though difficult to fully grasp how this works, we can see what the Bible says in Romans 5:

Verse 12, "...just as sin entered the world through one man, and death through sin..."

Verse 15, "...the many died by the trespass of the one man..."

Verse 16, "...The judgment followed one sin and brought condemnation..."

Verse 17, "...by the trespass of the one man, death [speaking of spiritual death] reigned through that one man..."

This is grim. However, in Romans 5:18-19 there is immense hope:

Consequently, just as the result of one trespass was con-demnation for all men, so also the result of one act of righteousness was justification that brings life for all men. For just as through the disobedience of the one man the many were made sinners, so also through the obedience of the one man the many will be made righteous.

When Adam and Eve decided to eat the forbidden fruit, in essence they were taking God (the King of kings) off the throne of their life and putting themselves on the throne. While this analogy has its limits, it is like that for us as well each time we choose to sin. Something has to change and it can—"...if anyone is in Christ, he is a new creation..." (2 Corinthians 5:17). We all need to have something change—even those who consider themselves to be good people. Our sin is not a flaw in God's work of creation. Actually, Ecclesiastes 7:29 says, "...God made mankind upright." However, original sin marked all of us with a heart disposed toward sin even before we actually committed sin. This inner sinfulness is the basic cause of the actual sins we commit. This is why it is true that "we are not sinners because we sin, but rather, we sin because we are sinners."

Starting and Finishing by Faith

We cannot earn forgiveness and salvation. It isn't like the old-time scales. In God's eyes, it isn't a case of good deeds out-weighing bad deeds. Biblical Christianity has no scale. Rather, "...there is now no condemnation for those who are in Christ Jesus, because through Christ Jesus the law of the Spirit of life set me free from the law of sin and death" (Romans 8:1-2). "For I am not ashamed of this Good News about Christ. It is the power of God at work, saving everyone who believes—Jews first and also Gentiles. This Good News tells us how God makes us right in His sight. This is accomplished *from start to finish by faith* (emphasis mine). As the Scriptures say, 'It is *through faith* that a righteous person has life' " (Romans 1:16-17 NLT) (emphasis mine). You'll read more about this "faith" in the next chapter.

The Billy Graham Evangelistic Association has produced a small booklet which explains what it means to invite Christ into our lives to take away our sins and give us eternal life. With gratitude and their blessing, the following is the primary contents of that booklet entitled:

"Steps to Peace with God"

Step 1: God's Purpose: Peace and Life...
God loves you and wants you to experience peace and life – abundant and eternal.
The Bible says...

"...we have peace with God through our Lord Jesus Christ." Romans 5:1

"For God so loved the world that he gave his one and only Son, that whoever believes in him shall not perish but have eternal life." John 3:16

"I have come that they may have life, and that they may have it more abundantly." John 10:10

Why don't most people have this peace and abundant life that God planned for us to have?

Step 2: The Problem: Our Separation...
God created us in His own image to have an abundant life. He did not make us robots to automatically love and obey Him. God gave us a will and freedom of choice.

We chose to disobey God and go our own willful way. We still make this choice today. This results in separation from God.

The Bible says...

"for all have sinned and fall short of the glory of God." Romans 3:23

"For the wages of sin is death, but the gift of God is eternal life in Christ Jesus our Lord." Romans 6:23

Our choice results in (sinful people's) separation from (a holy) God.

Our attempts to reach God
People have tried in many ways to bridge this gap between themselves and God...

The Bible says...

"There is a way that seems right to a man, but in the end it leads to death." Proverbs 14:12

"But your iniquities have separated you from your God; your sins have hidden his face from you, so that he will not hear." Isaiah 59:2

No bridge reaches God...except one
For a sinful person to reach a holy God, good works, religion, philosophy, morality, etc. will not provide that bridge.

Step 3: God's Bridge: The Cross...
Jesus Christ died on the Cross and rose from the grave. He paid the penalty for our sin and bridged the gap between God and people.

The Bible says...

"For there is one God and one mediator between God and men, the man Christ Jesus..." 1 Timothy 2:5

"For Christ died for sins once for all, the righteous for the unrighteous, to bring you to God." 1 Peter 3:18

"But God demonstrates his own love for us in this: While we were still sinners, Christ died for us." Romans 5:8

God has provided the only way…
Each person must make a choice…
The cross of Christ is God's provision of a bridge for sinful people to come to a holy God.

Step 4: Our Response: Receive Christ…
We must trust Jesus Christ as Lord and Savior and receive Him by personal invitation.

The Bible says…

"Here I am! I stand at the door and knock. If anyone hears my voice and opens the door, I will come in and eat with him, and he with me." Revelation 3:20

"Yet to all who received him, to those who believed in his name, he gave the right to become children of God." John 1:12

"That if you confess with your mouth, 'Jesus is Lord,' and believe in your heart that God raised him from the dead, you will be saved." Romans 10:9

Where are you?
Have you crossed over God's bridge?
Have you left your sin, rebellion, and separation from God by taking the bridge to God and received peace, forgiveness, abundant life, and eternal life?

Will you receive Jesus Christ now?

Here is how you can receive Christ:

1. *Admit your need (I am a sinner).*

2. *Be willing to turn from your sins (repent).*

3. *Believe that Jesus Christ died for you on the Cross and rose from the grave.*

4. *Through prayer, invite Jesus Christ to come in and control your life through the Holy Spirit (Receive Him as Lord and Savior).*

How to Pray:

Dear Lord Jesus,

I know that I am a sinner and need Your forgiveness. I believe that You died for my sins. I want to turn from my sins. I now invite You to come into my heart and life. I want to trust and follow You as Lord and Savior.

In Jesus' Name, Amen

God's Assurance: His Word

If you prayed this prayer, the Bible says…
"Everyone who calls on the name of the Lord will be saved."
Romans 10:13

Did you sincerely ask Jesus Christ to come into your life? Where is He right now? What has He given you?

The Bible says...

"For it is by grace you have been saved, through faith—and this not from yourselves, it is the gift of God—not by works, so that no one can boast." Ephesians 2:8-9

"He who has the Son has life; he who does not have the Son of God does not have life. I write these things to you who believe in the name of the Son of God so that you may know that you have eternal life." 1 John 5:12-13

Receiving Christ, we are born into God's family through the supernatural work of the Holy Spirit who indwells every believer. This is called regeneration or the "new birth."

This is just the beginning of a wonderful new life in Christ. To deepen this relationship you should:

1. *Read your Bible every day to know Christ better.*

2. *Talk to God in prayer every day.*

3. *Tell others about Christ.*

4. *Worship, fellowship, and serve with other Christians in a church where Christ is preached.*

5. *As Christ's representative in a needy world, demonstrate your new life by your love and concern for others.*

(Thanks to the Billy Graham Evangelistic Association and World Wide Publications for encouragement in quoting these words, which are now public domain. I hope they consider this use of these materials as an extension of their ministry).

Room for All Who Want to Come

Read Isaiah 55:1-2 for your encouragement.

Come, all you who are thirsty, come to the waters; and you who have no money, come, buy and eat! Come, buy wine and milk without money and without cost. Why spend money on what is not bread, and your labor on what does not satisfy? Listen, listen to me, and eat what is good, and your soul will delight in the richest of fare.

Many verses in the Bible tell us of the abundant life Christ gives to those who come to Him. Why is it that most do not avail themselves of this? Note the astonishing and extraordinary offer Jesus made to each of us in Matthew 11:28-30: "Come to me, all you who are weary and burdened, and I will give you rest. Take my yoke upon you and learn from me, for I am gentle and humble in heart, and you will find rest for your souls. For my yoke is easy and my burden is light."

Missionaries are sent because Christ is the only way of salvation. The reason we have Bible-centered, Christ-honoring churches across our nation and the world is because Christ is the only way of salvation. It is a narrow road, a small gate, and not many go through that gate and walk that road. However, this road to heaven has room for all who want to come to Christ.

We are urgent in our endeavor of spreading the Gospel. This has been true of committed followers of Christ since He lived, died, and rose from the dead while on earth and then ascended to His Father. So important is it that people hear of the only way of salvation that Christians have willingly given up family, friends, and even their own lives to tell others of Christ and the Good News of salvation through Christ. Combining this with the eternality of heaven makes the message of Christ the most important message in the world. This is the reason, many decades ago, missionaries put their lives at great risk to travel to far-off lands. Knowing there was a significant chance they would succumb to disease on the mission field in the tropics of Africa, some missionaries packed their belongings in a coffin. Their fervor to reach lost people was in light of their need to make a decision that would determine their eternal dwelling place.

There are unique aspects to the Gospel. Becoming a Christian begins a personal relationship with Christ. The reason this salvation is available to us is because, though we are all sinners by nature and by choice, God intervened on our behalf. We can enter a holy heaven because, when Christ died on the cross, He paid the complete price for our sins. He made us both sin-free and gave us His righteousness. We can, through this relationship with Christ, stand before God some day in the righteousness of Christ. Romans 4:7-8 explains this with an accounting metaphor: "Blessed are they whose transgressions are forgiven, whose sins are covered. Blessed is the man whose sin the Lord will never count against him." The word "count" here is an accounting word. No sin is listed in the ledger of liabilities for the believer.

Choosing Where to Spend Eternity

Everyone will spend eternity somewhere. There are only two choices. There is a place being prepared by Christ for the family of God called heaven. John 14:2-3 gives us a glimpse into the preparation that is now going on: "In my Father's house are many rooms; if it were not so, I would have told you. I am going there to prepare a place for you. And if I go and prepare a place for you, I will come back and take you to be with me that you also may be where I am." Revelation 21:1-4 gives us another glimpse:

> Then I saw a new heaven and a new earth, for the first heaven and the first earth had passed away, and there was no longer any sea. I saw the Holy City, the new Jerusalem, coming down out of heaven from God, prepared as a bride beautifully dressed for her husband. And I heard a loud voice from the throne saying, "Now the dwelling of God is with men, and he will live with them. They will be his people, and God himself will be with them and be their God. He will wipe every tear from their eyes. There will be no more death or mourning or crying or pain, for the old order of things has passed away."

There is another place being prepared. It is being prepared not for people, but for the devil and his angels. However, a multitude of people will be going there because it is the only alternative to heaven. Matthew 25:41 tells us about this other place: "Then he will say to those on his left, 'Depart from me, you who are cursed, into the eternal fire prepared for the devil and his angels.' " Another Scriptural insight is in Revelation 20:14-15: "Then death and Hades were thrown into the lake of fire. The lake of fire is the second death. If anyone's name was not found written in the book of life, he was thrown into the lake of fire."

I don't enjoy talking nor writing about hell or the lake of fire, but neither would I enjoy coming into your home in the middle of the night and telling you your house is on fire. However, while you would not enjoy being awakened suddenly with such bad news, you would be grateful I had done it. Knowing the truth is important in making our decisions on how we are going to live and it is important in what or whom we are going to trust with our eternal life.

We do not know a lot about either hell or heaven but we know enough to know hell is terrible beyond description and heaven is wonderful beyond description. Whether or not parts of what we read about these destinations are meant to be symbolic rather than literal, we can be assured that the awfulness of hell and wonders and glories of heaven are told us in language we can best understand by a God of truth, who is not given to exaggeration. Further, He knows the limits of our vocabulary and understanding.

God takes no delight in condemning a person to hell. God states this in Ezekiel 33:11: "As surely as I live, declares the Sovereign Lord, I take no pleasure in the death of the wicked, but rather that they turn from their ways and live." The death of Jesus Christ is adequate for all. We are told in 1 John 2:2, "He is the atoning sacrifice for our sins, and not only for ours but also for the sins of the whole world." That is good news!

What If You Only Think
You Are Going to Heaven?

People believing they are going to heaven but without having personally received Christ as Lord and Savior is a serious and widespread problem. I am neither judge nor jury but I do speak with people who believe they are going to heaven but who have not met the condition outlined in the Bible. Often they are not close to understanding what God says is the requirement of gaining eternal life. They may not have any idea of what Jesus meant when He said we must be "born again." Their concept of faith is often "faith in faith" rather than a personal faith in Jesus Christ as their Savior and Lord. He has asked that we receive Him and His gift of salvation. To believe is to receive, though many do not understand.

In our journey of assurance of salvation, we are wise to be certain we understand and have met the conditions for a personal relationship with Christ. Even good and sincere people can make assumptions and not understand the biblical way to eternal life. How tragic to not have met the conditions and to not know it!

We are fortunate to live in the era when Billy Graham served as America's evangelist. His little booklet, "Peace with God," clearly describes the biblical path to salvation. I've included it in this chapter.

It is a frightening thought that most people in America and around the world believe they are going to heaven, or at least to a better life, when their time on earth is over. Yet the Scriptures say only a few are prepared for heaven. Most are on their way to a Christ-less eternity. This chapter is written for these people. Whatever your relationship with Christ, I encourage you to study this chapter carefully even if you are certain you are on your way to an eternity with Christ. There is material here that you can use to help others.

There is surprising information in this chapter for many people. I remember my dad speaking with a cousin of mine about accepting Christ and asking for forgiveness based on His death on the cross. My cousin lived a good life and was sincere in telling my dad, "But I haven't done anything wrong." Dad explained we all sin; that we are born sinners. She later accepted Christ and now understands that she, like everyone, is a sinner and the only way of getting to heaven is through personal faith in Christ and receiving forgiveness through His death on the cross.

Some believe living a moral life and a life of good works earns us heaven. Others insist on tolerance. There are many ways we should be tolerant but one of them is not affirming a person's view of attaining heaven if it does not line up with what the Bible declares to be the only way. Like tolerance, sincerity is a virtue but it is not to be trusted in if we sincerely believe false information.

Think seriously about the issues of Chapter 3. If you have never come to repentance of sin and belief in Christ as Savior and Lord and have not received Him into your life by faith, this chapter is by far the most important in the entire book. While this book is about being assured we are going to heaven, defeating doubts, and confirming certainties, the beginning place is making a decision for Christ as detailed in this chapter. We gain what is of highest value when we receive Christ and lose nothing that is of great value. My plea to you and my prayer is that you come into a personal relationship with Christ as your Savior and Lord and are assured of heaven.

Personal Reflection or Discussion Questions

1. On what do you base your hope for eternal life in heaven?

2. Can you justify your answer to the first question with Scripture?

3. Are there any verses in the Bible that contradict your hope?

4. Is there any rational reason why a person would not place their faith in Christ? The price for salvation has been paid.

5. Consider this: Doing nothing is a decision against accepting Christ. A person has nothing of worth to lose by coming to Christ. They will receive a better life on earth and an eternity in heaven.

6. Is there any good reason why you will not make every reasonable effort to tell others about the eternal life offered by Christ?

Chapter 4

What Is Most Important in Gaining Eternal Life?

Acts 16:31

Romans 10:9-11

1 John 5:1

Just Believe

The Philippian jailer panicked. A violent earthquake struck and the prison doors flew open. Chains came loose and every prisoner was free to run. When the dust clouds settled, the jailer drew his sword and the Bible says he, "was about to kill himself because he thought the prisoners had escaped" (Acts 16:27). Responsible for these prisoners, he didn't want to face the Roman punishment for having allowed prisoners to escape.

Just then, Paul shouted, "Don't harm yourself! We are all here!" (Acts 16:28). The jailer, who must have been astonished to see two men still in the jail, as well as overcome by what he experienced, responded, "Sirs, what must I do to be saved?" Paul and Silas answered, "Believe in the Lord Jesus, and you will be saved" (Acts 16:31). In that moment the jailer believed and was saved.

He believed "in the Lord Jesus." Is belief all there is to being saved or does becoming a Christian take more than that? Let's take the best-known Bible verse and look for answers. "For God so loved the world that he gave his one and only Son, that whoever believes in him shall not perish but have eternal life" (John 3:16). Are there other verses like this? Many! One exercise for you to do to clarify the importance of "belief" in Christianity is to record in a notebook all the verses in the New Testament that use the word "believe." A concordance can help you do that. Clearly, "believe" is the transaction. It's the truth of Scripture declared over and over.

In my own experience with doubt, I thought I needed to do more than believe—like pray a certain way, use just the right words, and have just the right amount of faith and enough sincerity. But I couldn't measure words, faith, or sincerity so I never knew if they were enough.

We are saved by believing in Christ. I understood this truth better when I put myself in the place of those who lived in the time of Christ. Nazareth, where Jesus grew up, wasn't much of a town. Even Nathanael exclaimed, "Nazareth! Can anything good come from there?" (John 1:46). Joseph, Jesus' earthly step-father, was a carpenter—a vocation that allowed him to make an honest living but didn't take his family to the top strata of society. They were probably middle class. The Jews had looked forward to the Messiah's coming for centuries. They wanted someone to deliver them, and now someone from the lowly town of Nazareth claimed to be that person! Even Jesus' family found His claims of being the Messiah hard to believe, just as it would be hard for us to believe our brother was the Messiah.

> Coming to his hometown, he began teaching the people in their synagogue, and they were amazed. "Where did this man get this wisdom and these miraculous powers?" they asked. "Isn't this the carpenter's son? Isn't his mother's name Mary, and aren't his brothers James, Joseph, Simon and Judas? Aren't all his sisters with us? Where then did this man get all these things?" And they took offense at him (Matthew 13:54-57).

John 7:5 says, "Even his own brothers did not believe in him."

We benefit from centuries of accounts of lives changed through faith in Christ. The Scriptures, written and handed down to us, prophecies fulfilled (more on that later), and so much more make it easier for us to believe that Jesus is our Savior. However, the criteria for being a child of God is the same—believe. I am not talking about something small or insignificant. I'm writing about something simple that changes our lives and determines where we will spend eternity. The benefit is colossal, yet our side of the transaction is simple.

Think of all the verses in Scripture that state those who believe in Christ are forgiven. My favorite illustration of belief and salvation comes from Harry Ironside's *Epistles of John and Jude*. While I worked from the 11th printing, the first one was in 1931. He was quoting from, and commenting on, 1 John 5:13,

King James Version. He wrote:

> Do you believe on the name of the Son of God? It is not
> an intellectual thing of which he speaks. Do you have
> faith in the Son of God? Do you trust in Him? Listen,
> then; I have a message for you, and I wish it would come
> home to every heart with power as if you had never heard
> it before. Suppose a letter came, and on its envelope you
> read, "To you who believe on the name of the Son of
> God." I say, "A letter has been handed to me, and if the
> person to whom it is addressed is here, please come claim
> it. It is addressed to 'You who believe.'" What would you
> say? Do you believe on the name of the Son of God? Is
> the letter for you? Very well, then; let us open and see
> what it says. "That ye may know that ye have eternal life,
> even you who believe on the name of the Son of God."
> It is a message from the high court of heaven to every
> believer in the Lord Jesus Christ. Have you been doubt-
> ing all through the years…hoping all the while that you
> are heaven-bound, but not very sure of it? Get it settled
> today, put away your doubts and fears, and look by faith
> at the risen Christ. Take it from the blessed God Him-
> self that "He that believeth on the Son hath everlasting
> life." (Harry Ironside, *Epistles of John and Jude*. Loizeaux
> Brothers Inc., 1969)

Would you step forward and take a letter addressed "To you
who believe in the name of the Son of God?" Do you believe in
the name of the Son of God?

I believed. Regardless if you or I know the day we first believed in Christ or not, regardless of whether you had big faith or little faith, whether or not we understood much or little of what we were doing—the issue is do you "believe in the name of the Son of God?" Could you claim that envelope? If so, God is telling you in His Word that you can "know that you have eternal life." You have the envelope. You have the message from God. Don't let Satan cause you to doubt anymore.

When I invited Christ into my life at age five, I didn't understand the theology of the Bible, nor did I need to. I accepted all I knew and my heels were not dug in on the areas I didn't understand. I came with my nothingness to receive His everything. I came with what little I knew and received Christ in all His fullness. I believed. After all, Jesus said in Luke 18:17, "I tell you the truth, anyone who will not receive the kingdom of God like a little child will never enter it." I knew very little but I came. I accepted the gift of salvation as best I understood.

Pisteuo (anglicized spelling) in the Greek New Testament is regularly used in the New Testament for "believe." This word is used in 1 John 5:13 as well as in the jail episode at Philippi (Acts 16:31). In the New Testament, *pisteuo* appears in the noun form 239 times and in the adjective form 52 times. This means, on average, a form of this word appears twice in every chapter of the New Testament. The litmus test of salvation is—are you trusting Christ?

Faith Alone

How does an understanding of belief strengthen our assurance? Salvation is by faith in Christ alone—faith plus nothing.

The primary theme of the book of Galatians is this very thing: salvation is by faith alone. There were those who said, "Yes, salvation is by faith in Christ but one also has to…," and they added something to faith. Paul writes strongly about this in Galatians 3:1-5:

> You foolish Galatians! Who has bewitched you?…Did you receive the Spirit by observing the law, or by believing what you heard? Are you so foolish? After beginning with the Spirit, are you now trying to attain your goal by human effort?…Does God give you his Spirit and work miracles among you because you observe the law, or because you believe what you heard?

 In the Reformation, Martin Luther used the phrase *Sola Fide* (faith alone). Look at Romans 1:17: "For in the gospel a righteousness from God is revealed, a righteousness that is by faith from first to last, just as it is written: 'The righteous will live by faith.'" Faith and believing are synonymous. Does understanding this change anything in our lives? Yes, an amazing thing happens. We are "born again." Just as we were born the first time with a birth of flesh, now we are born again, this time with a birth of the Spirit. This changes our lives to the extent that Scripture says we become new creatures in Christ. Second Corinthians 5:17 states, "Therefore, if anyone is in Christ, he is a new creation; the old has gone, the new has come!" Place beside this striking verse 1 Corinthians 6:19: "Do you not know that your body is a temple of the Holy Spirit, who is in you, whom you have received from God"? God is living in you. As has been said, "When you go to the store, God goes to the store…our task is to carry God around." We simply believe and then we are a child of God with God the Holy Spirit living inside our bodies.

Belief Determines Actions

With our bodies being the temple of the Holy Spirit, we have a source of power to change our behaviors. Paul speaks of "the obedience that comes from faith" (Romans 1:5). The eleventh chapter of Hebrews repeatedly shows a close link between belief and obedience.

One Sunday morning after preaching at two services and having our typical and varied conversations with people, Dee and I drove out of the parking lot and headed down the street until we came to a red light. It stayed red for a long time, although it probably seemed longer because we were tired. Our patience wore thin and Dee said, "Let's just go. It's broken." I accelerated and pronto—red and blue flashing lights were right behind our car. Unimpressed with our explanation that the light was broken, the police officer invited us to watch it change colors. We believed the light mechanism was broken. If what one believes is not true, his or her belief has no value. I have several traffic tickets, including one from that day, to prove that what I believed to be true was wrong. Regardless of my explanations and my false belief, I helped underwrite the city budget that day. I must bring my belief system of what the laws say and mean into alignment with truth.

Belief determines what we do or don't do. For example, if I believe someone will shoot me if I walk out of my house, I will stay inside. If I know my car's radiator is empty and by driving it the engine will be ruined, I will add radiator fluid or not drive the car. If I believe a nuclear bomb will be dropped on my city next week, I will tell others, leave the city, and travel to a safe place.

Let's transfer this principle to salvation. If you believe Christ will come into your life, take away your sins and give you eternal life, and you believe His way is best, you will come to Christ. Belief determines actions.

Belief determining action is a profound insight, not only in relationship to Christ and salvation, but also in relationship to life itself. Belief in God requires serious thought because belief determines action. This is of major significance. It is life changing— "...to all who received him, to those who believed in his name, he gave the right to become children of God" (John 1:12). Is it extreme to think everything we do is determined by what we believe? Not at all—even the self-help industry acknowledges that belief determines action. So it is with salvation. It is not "just" faith. The door to heaven opens through faith in what is *true*. Not every road leads to heaven. Jesus said in John 14:6, "I am *the* way and *the* truth and *the* life. No one comes to the Father except through me" (emphasis mine). He uses the definite article "the." Acts 4:12 says it this way: "Salvation is found in no one else, for there is *no other name* under heaven given to men by which we must be saved" (emphasis mine). It is exclusive but it is also available to all who wish to come. The Bible's last chapter, verse 17, says the invitation to salvation continues with, "...whoever wishes, let him take the free gift of the water of life." The invitation is to whoever wishes. They can partake of the unspeakable blessings of heaven as freely as we might drink from a fresh stream. Salvation is exclusive, but wide open to "whoever wishes."

When you place your faith in Christ, your name is supernaturally written in the Lamb's Book of Life, which is the directory of heaven. The New Testament makes six references to this, including one in Philippians 4 and five in Revelation.

Following our entry into a relationship with Christ, the Holy Spirit begins to produce His fruit within us, just as a mature apple tree produces apples. This spiritual fruit is listed in Galatians 5:22-23: "But the fruit of the Spirit is love, joy, peace, patience, kindness, goodness, faithfulness, gentleness and self-control." We produce fruit when we place our trust in Christ as Savior and Lord; because it is at that time the Holy Spirit begins to produce the likeness of Christ in our lives. The challenge of Christian living is allowing the Holy Spirit to bring our day-to-day living in line with our position in Christ and with His purposes for our life.

Most Americans believe that Jesus existed and lived in Nazareth. But believing in Christ is not just an intellectual belief in a historical Jesus who called Himself the Christ, the Messiah, and the Son of God. A genuine belief in Christ includes a belief that responds to what He says, which is to receive Him personally as the one who paid the penalty for their sins, and to follow Him as their Lord and master. Do you believe? Or, put another way, are you trusting in Christ for forgiveness of sins and eternal life with Him? If so, you can *know* you are going to heaven! For those who believe but lack the confidence they are going to heaven, remember that God said belief in Him is the path to salvation and Scripture tells us we can know we are going to heaven.

Imagine the fear filling those who believe they cannot know

until the day they stand before God whether they will enter heaven or be cast into hell? I want to know before I reach the end of my life—before it is too late to do anything about it. God has an envelope with your name on it. Open it. If you are a believer, you can *know* you have eternal life. I love helping people have clarity on the issues of faith and belief and, with that I am including one more verse. This one is from Philippians 3:9: "and be found in him, not having a righteousness of my own that comes from the law, but that which is through faith in Christ—the righteousness that comes from God and is by faith."

Summary of Chapter 4

What Is Most Important in Gaining Eternal Life?

During my years of doubt, the biblical understanding in this chapter was so helpful to me that many of you may ask, "Why did you still doubt? Didn't you know this information?" The answer is both yes and no. If you had asked me if the contents of this chapter are true, I would have said, "Yes." However, internalizing it—as opposed to being concerned that I had prayed "right," or was sincere enough, or had enough faith, or had not committed the unpardonable sin—confused me. It should not have; but it did.

There are two statements in the Bible that give great comfort as to the simplicity of coming to Christ. He did not make it hard. He made it easy. He said we are to come as a child (Mark 10:15). And then, He said we come by faith, trust, and belief (Romans 1:17). It isn't an ordeal like TV's *Jeopardy* or an episode of *Survivor*.

Jesus wants us to come. He has paid the price for our coming. He invites with words like, "Come to me, all you who are weary and burdened, and I will give you rest. Take my yoke upon you and learn from me, for I am gentle and humble in heart, and you will find rest for your souls. For my yoke is easy and my burden is light" (Matthew 11:28-30). I have ridden in an ox cart pulled by two oxen working together with one double yoke. I know what they do and the importance of the oxen working together and the yoke being a good fit. Whoever you are and whatever your circumstances, there is a "Jesus-yoke" for you. One of the meanings of "easy" in verse 20 is "fits." His yoke fits you. It is custom-made for you by Jesus. Along with a yoke that fits, He wants to give you rest for your soul.

Do you want Jesus, eternal life, a yoke that fits, rest for your soul, and so much more? You can have it. Christ is knocking at the door of your heart, asking for permission to come in. It opens from the inside. I'm glad when I came to Christ, He didn't ask me to attend seminary first nor grill me on biblical or systematic theology. He didn't make me jump through difficult hoops. He just wanted me to put my simple trust in Him for eternal salvation.

Personal Reflection or Discussion Questions

1. What is belief?

2. How does belief differ from an academic or "head knowledge" of Christ and the plan of salvation?

3. What are the indications of true belief?

4. Why is there confusion over the way of salvation when the Bible is clear?

5. How do repentance, church membership, and good works relate to salvation?

6. How can one have complete assurance of salvation?

Chapter 5

Can You Know You Are Not Guilty of the Unpardonable Sin?

Matthew 12:22-32

Mark 3:22-30

Luke 12:8-10

The Unpardonable Sin

I'm sure I'm not alone when I say I feared I had committed "the unpardonable sin," which the Bible says, "...will not be forgiven, either in this age or in the age to come" (Matthew 12:32). I was in upper elementary school when a buddy and I were talking as we rode our bikes. I remember him saying, "Do you know there is a sin God won't forgive?" I had accepted Christ and, as a preacher's kid, I was in church several times a week but did not remember hearing there was an unforgivable sin. My quick response to my friend was, "No there isn't—God will forgive all sins." He insisted on his position and I insisted on mine. When I got home I asked my mother. Her reply was cautious, perhaps because she knew the way I was wired. "There is a sin God won't forgive," she said, "but it is nothing you need to worry about." But I did worry about it—a lot and for many years.

In a complementary way, this unpardonable sin is recorded in all the synoptic Gospels:

Matthew 12:22-32

Then they brought him a demon-possessed man who was blind and mute, and Jesus healed him, so that he could both talk and see. All the people were astonished and said, "Could this be the Son of David?" But when the Pharisees heard this, they said, "It is only by Beelzebub, the prince of demons, that this fellow drives out demons." Jesus knew their thoughts and said to them, "Every kingdom divided against itself will be ruined, and every city or household divided against itself will not stand. If Satan drives out Satan, he is divided against himself. How then can his kingdom stand? And if I drive out demons by Beelzebub, by whom do your people drive them out? So then, they will be your judges. But if I drive out demons by the Spirit of God, then the kingdom of God has come upon you. Or again, how can anyone enter a strong man's house and carry off his possessions unless he first ties up the strong man? Then he can rob his house. He who is not with me is against me, and he who does not gather with me scatters. And so I tell you, every sin and blasphemy will be forgiven men, but the blasphemy against the Spirit will not be forgiven. Anyone who speaks a word against the Son of Man will be forgiven, but anyone who speaks against the Holy Spirit will not be forgiven, either in this age or in the age to come."

Mark 3:22-30
And the teachers of the law who came down from Jerusalem said, "He is possessed by Beelzebub! By the prince of demons he is driving out demons." So Jesus called them and spoke to them in parables: "How can Satan drive out Satan? If a kingdom is divided against itself, that kingdom cannot stand. If a house is divided against itself, that house cannot stand. And if Satan opposes himself and is divided, he cannot stand; his end has come. In fact, no one can enter a strong man's house and carry off his possessions unless he first ties up the strong man. Then he can rob his house. I tell you the truth, all the sins and blasphemies of men will be forgiven them. But whoever blasphemes against the Holy Spirit will never be forgiven; he is guilty of an eternal sin." He said this because they were saying, "He has an evil spirit."

Luke 12:8-10
"I tell you, whoever acknowledges me before men, the Son of Man will also acknowledge him before the angels of God. But he who disowns me before men will be disowned before the angels of God. And everyone who speaks a word against the Son of Man will be forgiven,

but anyone who blasphemes against the Holy Spirit will not be forgiven."

What a journey I began that day! I read the above passages over and over trying to figure out "the blasphemy against the Holy Spirit." Then I went to my dad's library and began researching Bible commentaries. To my surprise and dismay, they didn't agree. I learned all the major views but, because there were differing views by excellent scholars of Scripture, I concluded no one really knew what the unpardonable sin was. If no one knows what the unpardonable sin is, how could I know I hadn't committed it? I anguished as I thought about being in hell forever and I was more scared than I had ever been—to a degree that can't be expressed in words.

The most common views of the "unpardonable sin" are:

1. It is attributing the work of the Holy Spirit or of Christ to Satan.

2. It is the constant, complete, and final rejection of the Holy Spirit drawing a person to Christ. A verse such as Proverbs 29:1, "A man who remains stiff-necked after many rebukes will suddenly be destroyed—without remedy," could give a hint of this. Further, inasmuch as it is the Holy Spirit who draws a person to Christ, if a person makes an ultimate, complete, and final rejection of the Holy Spirit's drawing them to Christ, they have removed themselves from the opportunity to accept Christ.

3. A modification of the above view is that, while the rejection

persists, the Holy Spirit is being blasphemed. If the person changes and responds to the Holy Spirit, their sins are forgiven and they are saved. This view teaches that the issue is not God's unwillingness to forgive them; but that they are unwilling to come to Christ.

4. A fourth view is that the unpardonable sin could not be committed except during Christ's incarnation (physically on earth).

The first view, that the unpardonable sin is attributing the work of the Holy Spirit or of Christ to Satan, strikes a chord from our own lives. Sometimes we see something terrible happen and we may say, or at least believe, that it came from the hand of Satan. Who of us hasn't ignorantly attributed to Satan something God did Himself? With God, who knows everything and works in the eternal realm, things that appear to be negative may have been designed by Him for a sacred purpose. The Old Testament gives many examples of horrific events that came from the hand of God, even though at times He used Satan to carry them out.

Regarding the second view, if a person will not accept Christ and, consequently, the person dies in his or her sin, their sins are not forgiven. That does not mean there was a particular sin they committed which was unpardonable.

Regarding the third view, if a person comes to Christ, their prior refusal to do so isn't unpardonable. It is debatable whether or not this position should be in this list because for one who has committed this sin, then comes to Christ, the sin is forgiven and is no longer unpardonable.

The fourth view, since it pertains to the 33 years of Christ's incarnate (dwelling in a human body) state on earth, would not apply to us today.

Which of these views is correct? Maybe none of them. The truth may be a blending of several interpretations.

How Do We Deal with the Unpardonable Sin?

What should a person do if he or she is concerned about having committed the sin the Bible calls "unpardonable"? Only God knows the strain of those years when I was consumed with fear that I had committed the unpardonable sin. Though I didn't believe I had committed this sin, and I didn't know what it was, the stakes were so high that, again, even a one percent chance I had committed it was too much for me to have peace and joy. A one percent chance of going to hell and not being able to get out plagued me like nothing else. As others with this struggle, I had difficulty living the abundant life Christ offered.

My dear mother and dad gave me the help that worked for most people. I continued to read anything I could find on the subject. Several years after I expressed my fears to my parents, I talked with a nationally known scholar. He added little to what I already knew. He assured me I was on my way to heaven—that I had not committed the unpardonable sin. I appreciated his genuine love and patience. He was a brilliant and famous biblical scholar and, from my perspective, I had never met a godlier man. However, because of my own upside-down thinking, I didn't find his comments persuasive. This was devastating as there was no one in the world whose opinion I respected more than my parents and this man. "Who could help me now?" I wondered.

I pursued a new path. It was a turn-around experience. It pointed me in the direction I needed to find my way out of this fear. One part of this new direction was my understanding that if a person is concerned about the unpardonable sin in their life, that in itself is an indication they are not guilty of this sin.

You might ask, what if a person wants to come to Christ for salvation but is afraid they have committed the unpardonable sin? Well, it's like asking, "What if a dead man got up and walked?" The answer is, "He wasn't dead." So if a person fears they have committed the unpardonable sin and now want to come to Christ, they can come. They haven't committed the unpardonable sin. How do I know? I know because this view is consistent with all the verses that invite a person to come to Christ. These verses are without any parenthetical statements such us "unless they have committed the unpardonable sin."

Here's the key. Instead of trying to figure out what the unpardonable sin was, I followed the path of how to know I had *not* committed this sin. This is where I found victory by the leading and confirmation of the Holy Spirit through His Word. And, so can you! The key is to know we have not committed the unpardonable sin, not in worrying about the definition of what it is. And so again, we go to the Scriptures because it is the truth that sets us free (John 8:32). I can't tell you how liberating this new track was for me.

One of the simple, clear, and powerful verses my mother gave me was Romans 10:13: "Everyone who calls on the name of the Lord will be saved." She said, "Did you call?" I said, "Yes." She said, "Then you are saved." And with Dad, many things were appropriately either black or white. If Romans 10:13 says, "Everyone who calls on the name of the Lord will be saved," then that was the way it was. No ifs, ands, or buts. I wished I could be more like my dad.

Keys to Interpreting the Bible

A key insight into biblical interpretation is that, properly understood, no verse in Scripture makes another verse untrue. Every verse stands—no exceptions. It is the Word of the Lord. Psalm 12:6 says, "...the words of the Lord are flawless, like silver refined in a furnace of clay, purified seven times." Revelation 22:18-19 warns us to not add or take away from the Word of God.

Many verses can help you know that you are, in fact, a forgiven child of God. John 6:37 says, "...whoever comes to me I will never drive away." Have you come to Christ? He does not drive away those who come. If you desire to come to Christ, that is proof that you have not committed the unpardonable sin. The Bible is its own best interpreter but the truth of one verse does not cancel out the truth of another verse.

Perhaps the favorite verse of the church of Christ is John 3:16: "For God so loved the world that he gave his one and only Son, that whoever believes in him shall not perish but have eternal life." Do you believe in Christ? If you believe you have eternal life, you will not perish. This is true regardless of what you have done. It is proof that you have not committed the unpardonable sin. There is no parenthetical statement after "whoever" which says, "unless you have committed the unpardonable sin." The

Apostle Paul said in 1 Timothy 1:15, "…Christ Jesus came into the world to save sinners—of whom I am the worst." When Paul believed in Christ, he received eternal life and gave proof, by his belief, that he had not committed the unpardonable sin despite his opinion he was "the worst."

Continuing on this liberating track, more verses will confirm your assurance. John 1:12 says, "…to all who received him, to those who believed in his name, he gave the right to become children of God," and Revelation 22:17, "The Spirit and the bride say, 'Come!' And let him who hears say, 'Come!' Whoever is thirsty, let him come; and whoever wishes, let him take the free gift of the water of life." What wording could make the way of salvation more open to everyone who wants to be saved than "whoever wishes"? Do you want to come? Then you can. The fact you *want* to come is proof that you have not committed the unpardonable sin.

This leads us to a bigger view of Scripture. There's a danger of believing one passage of Scripture as true—but modifying another passage as having limited or partial authority in light of another verse. We do this because we cannot, with our finite minds, put it all together. But, God is not finite—He is infinite. He can do all things and He knows all things which makes 1 John 5:13 possible: "I write these things…that you may know that you have eternal life." Because He says we can know, we can know!

Remember that no verse of Scripture makes another verse untrue or less true. This can be your way out whether your struggle is with the unpardonable sin or with any personal sin you have difficulty believing God will forgive. In one of my Bibles, I had written regarding Revelation 22:17, "I don't understand the unpardonable sin but I do understand when Christ says 'whoever wills—or desires—let him take...freely' " and I wanted it! Matthew 12, Mark 3, and Luke 12 are true and do not take away from Revelation 22:17 which is also true. Neither reference takes anything away from another reference. All four passages are completely true—without any qualification, just as Romans 10:13 and John 6:37 (and a host of other verses) do not take away from God's warning of an unpardonable sin.

Reflect on the following verses and brief comments:

John 6:37: "...whoever comes to me I will never drive away."

What did He promise to all who come to Him? Did He qualify His invitation regarding those who come to Him? Do you believe this is true for others but not for you? Why would you be the only exception?

Romans 10:13: "Everyone who calls on the name of the Lord will be saved."

Have you called on the name of the Lord to save you? If you were serious, you were saved.

You may be wondering if you called on the Lord with enough faith. The fact you even called, as weak as your faith was, that was enough faith. If you had no faith at all, you would not have bothered to call. If you called, you will be among those Christ takes with Him to heaven when He returns. If you die before He returns, you will be resurrected with the rest of the saints and spend eternity with Him (1 Thessalonians 4:13-18).

We are all born sinners and that is the reason we sin. We don't become sinners *by* sinning, we *were already* sinners. Romans 3:10-13 (much like Psalm 14:1-3 and Psalm 53:1-3) tells us that by nature none of us seek after God. What makes us even want to come to Christ? John 6:44 says, "No one can come to me unless the Father who sent me draws him." Jeremiah 31:3, "The Lord appeared to us in the past, saying: 'I have loved you with an everlasting love; I have drawn you with loving-kindness.' "

There is nothing good in us, nothing in us by nature that would cause us to want to come to Christ. If God the Father did not draw us, we'd have no desire to come. Thank God He wanted to draw us to Himself! This should give us confidence and assurance as well as cause for rejoicing. Without understanding all there is to know about God drawing us to salvation, or why some are drawn and others are not, we should take what we *do* understand and leave the things we don't understand to a merciful, just, and loving God.

Can You Know You Are Not Guilty of the Unpardonable Sin?

The more I studied the unpardonable sin in Matthew 12, Mark 3, and Luke 12, the more I was confused. How could I know I hadn't committed it if scholars couldn't agree on what it is? Commentaries present at least four views. I studied them all and I had good counsel, but I couldn't settle it.

Why? Did I really think I had committed this unpardonable sin? No. The primary dilemma was the size of the issue. The odds were in my favor. But, even if there was a one percent chance I had committed this dreadful sin and would be in the Lake of Fire forever, the situation was unacceptable because the stakes were so high.

After a great amount of study over a period of years, I concluded it was not possible to definitively determine what the unpardonable sin was. Consequently, my new direction, and I concluded it was the right direction, was to seek to find a way of determining I hadn't committed this sin, whatever it was. I found I had a clear track to run on, a large number of scriptural passages to give support. I was on my way to victory! The truth was setting me free.

Contributing to my assurance of salvation was knowing that no verse in Scripture makes another verse untrue. John 6:37 says that the Lord will not cast out anyone who comes to Him and no other Scripture can take this truth away. Also, this is true regardless of what a person has done—there are no parentheses or qualifiers in John 3:16: "For God so loved the world that he gave his one and only Son, that whoever believes in him shall not perish but have eternal life."

Personal Reflection or Discussion Questions

1. Summarize how you can know you have not committed the unpardonable sin.

2. Is there anything in the way of knowing you are a Christian?

3. Recite a favorite verse of assurance. Then tell why this is a favorite.

4. Is there something else you need to know in order to understand you can come to Christ and, by coming, know you have not committed the unpardonable sin?

5. Is there ever a reason a person who wants to come to Christ cannot come?

6. Is it clear to you that the fact you want to know Christ in a personal way is proof you have not committed the unpardonable sin?

Chapter 6

Can You Sin So Much You Cannot Come to Christ?

Hebrews 6:4-9, 10:26-27

Making Peace with Difficult Verses

Rich was desperate. He was in the living room of a pastor-friend of mine pouring out his heart. Though his wife had recently divorced him, his finances were in ruin, and he was in trouble with the law, none of those things had driven him to seek help. What had brought him to a counseling session with this pastor was his awful fear that his sins were too great for God's forgiveness. Though he had prayed the prayer of salvation a number of times, he didn't "feel" part of God's family because of his terrible guilt over some things he had done. The doubts about where he would spend eternity consumed him and filled him with fear. "I can face everything else in life if I can just resolve this one question: Could God still accept me?" he asked.

As we turn our attention to the question of whether those who have sinned a great deal can still be forgiven, you will learn and be assured that the answer is a big, God-made, wonderful "Yes!" Admittedly, we will be dealing with difficult biblical passages. Most of the Bible is easy to understand and interpret; but some passages take serious study to determine their meaning. And there are a few passages that no one can fully understand. Remember, "The secret things belong to the Lord our God" (Deuteronomy 29:29). With the Bible as our authority and the Holy Spirit as our teacher, it is an adventure of blessing and joy to "dig in" and do our best to understand God's Word. I encourage you to make this a regular part of your life.

The central question of this chapter, the one Rich and many others, including myself, struggled with—can you sin so much you cannot come to Christ?—has us examining Hebrews 6 and 10.

Hebrews 6:4-9:

> (4) It is impossible for those who have once been enlightened, who have tasted the heavenly gift, who have shared in the Holy Spirit, (5) who have tasted the goodness of the word of God and the powers of the coming age, (6) if they fall away, to be brought back to repentance, because to their loss they are crucifying the Son of God all over again and subjecting him to public disgrace. (7) Land that drinks in the rain often falling on it and that produces a crop useful to those for whom it is farmed

receives the blessing of God. (8) But land that produces thorns and thistles is worthless and is in danger of being cursed. In the end it will be burned. (9) Even though we speak like this, dear friends, we are confident of better things in your case—things that accompany salvation.

Whether the writer of the book of Hebrews was speaking to Christians or non-Christians, as a boy I was afraid this passage was speaking to me. It was not hard for me to imagine I was an "impossible" case because I had been enlightened; I had experienced the heavenly gift (salvation). I had shared in the Holy Spirit and I had tasted of the goodness of the Word of God. I didn't know, however, much about "the powers of the coming age." If it was speaking of me, I was hopeless and helpless and, at that point in my young life, I didn't want to tell my fears to anyone.

Once again I explored Dad's library. Was Hebrews 6 speaking about people who had come to Christ or those who had not? Views among theologians varied. To some extent it seemed to parallel the Arminian and Calvinistic positions (See Appendix). Because there were good scholars on both sides, these books were little to no help.

Impossible to Come Back

Back to the text, in verse 4, the phrase "It is impossible" is a clear statement. Whatever they had done, whoever was being spoken of, it was impossible "to be brought back to repentance." Why is it impossible? God can do all things (Matthew

19:26). Is it because God would refuse this person if they sought repentance?

The impossibility of this person's situation was not on God's part. This would contradict the Scriptures, such as John 6:37: "...whoever comes to me I will never drive away." At the same time we don't have the option of taking lightly or diminishing the word "impossible." Nor should we permit our theology to get in the way of this verse—allow the Scriptures to declare their truths!

While God can do all things, the person described in Hebrews 6:4 is someone who, apparently, had so hardened his heart it was impossible for him to come back. The issue is not that God could not or would not let him come back but rather he had so hardened himself he would not come back. He was unwilling "to be brought back to repentance" (verse 6). How do I conclude this? Simply because of the abundance of verses, many already quoted, which say anyone who wants to come to Christ, can come. This person, not God, had shut the door. This person, in his own obstinate way, arrived at by his own ungodly decisions, had made a final choice. The impossibility lay in the person who had closed the door to God's only plan of salvation.

This warning has an immediate application. If a person is falling farther and farther away from where God wants him or her to be, spiritual calluses thickening, sensitivity to spiritual things fading, that individual should be deeply concerned. He or she is creating distance from God, perhaps entering the situation mentioned in the Old Testament: "A man who remains stiff-necked after many rebukes will suddenly be destroyed—without remedy" (Proverbs 29:1). It is fair warning to all of us. It is a broad, sweeping statement put there by the inspiration of God.

Scripture is not meant to be sugar-coated, causing us to simply have a "feel good" religion. It does not say we will all end up in the same place regardless of what we do or do not believe. We must not allow ourselves to reject anything of Scripture or of the Spirit's working in our life because it causes us discomfort. True salvation from God is exclusive. It comes only through Christ. Though exclusive, it remains available to everyone who wants to come to Christ.

Recall with me, Isaiah 66:5: "Hear the word of the Lord, you who tremble at his word." That was not sugar-coated. People trembled at God's words. Just this morning I read Psalm 99:1: "The Lord reigns, let the nations tremble; he sits enthroned between the cherubim, let the earth shake." Rather than reading quickly past hard and negative verses and only looking at the ones that make us feel good, we should read them in balance with each other. All of God's Word is important.

All Who Want to Come, Can

There is good news here. These verses in Hebrews 6 have nothing to do with people who fear they are guilty. The fact a person is concerned establishes they are not the ones who have fallen away beyond the possibility of being "brought back." If anyone wants to repent and return to the Savior, they can. As mentioned before, the Bible is its own best interpreter. We bring all Scripture to bear on all of Scripture to the extent we are able.

How do we deal with this passage in a way that is both consistent with the rest of Scripture and part of our being assured of going to heaven? Let's look at verses that establish who are the true believers. The psalmist said clearly, "...the words of the Lord are flawless, like silver refined in a furnace of clay, purified seven times" (Psalm 12:6). Look at 2 Timothy 3:16-17: "All Scripture is God-breathed and is useful for teaching, rebuking, correcting and training in righteousness, so that the man of God may be thoroughly equipped for every good work." However, that does not dismiss the warning of Hebrews 6:4-6. Here, as with the unpardonable sin, we remember the verses telling us anyone who wants to come to Christ *can* come. There are no exceptions to this, regardless of what sins people have committed.

> John 3:16: "For God so loved the world that he gave his one and only Son, that whoever believes in him shall not perish but have eternal life."

> Romans 10:13: "Everyone who calls on the name of the Lord will be saved."

> John 6:37: "...whoever comes to me I will never drive away."

> John 1:12: "...to all who received him, to those who believed in his name, he gave the right to become children of God."

> Revelation 22:17: "The Spirit and the bride say, 'Come!' And let him who hears say, 'Come!' Whoever is thirsty, let him come; and whoever wishes, let him take the free gift of the water of life."

All of this leads to the understanding that the reason the person described in Hebrews 6 is in an impossible situation is because of his or her own falling away and recalcitrant attitude toward coming back to Christ. If you are afraid you are one of these people, you prove you are not if you come to Christ in repentance and faith. Do you believe this? I know the word "impossible" is a chilling word—it scared me!

But look at these verses, study them, meditate upon them, memorize them, and lay them over your deepest fears. It gets down to this—do you believe in the complete inspiration of Scripture? I am not asking if you think the writers of Scripture were perfect and infallible. The question is—do you believe a perfect God would write an imperfect book? Do you believe His inspiration of these writers and the supervision of their writing was less than complete? Reexamine Psalm 12:6 and 2 Timothy 3:16-17. Then cross-reference these verses with other places in Scripture where the absolute reliability of Scripture is clear.

Don't be discouraged. Even Peter had trouble understanding some of what Paul wrote. Peter writes in 2 Peter 3:16: "…His [speaking of Paul] letters contain some things that are hard to understand." While we do not know everything this passage in Hebrews 6 teaches (just as we don't know all that is embodied in the passages on the unpardonable sin), we can still find assurance that we have eternal life. Our study in *Assured of Heaven* is based upon the authority of the Bible. Allow this repetition to underline in your mind that while we do not know for sure what the unpardonable sin is and what the sin of Hebrews 6 is, we can know we have not committed them. A great number of verses tell us how we can know we have eternal life. Be assured of heaven!

There Is Only One Plan

Let's move on. Note the serious situation of these people who:

...have once been enlightened, who have tasted the heavenly gift, who have shared in the Holy Spirit, who have tasted the goodness of the word of God and the powers of the coming age, if they fall away...to their loss they are crucifying the Son of God all over again and subjecting him to public disgrace (Hebrews 6:4-6).

Their crime was heinous. These people had effectively excluded themselves from the only plan of salvation available to humanity. Having had those spiritual benefits mentioned in verses 4 and 5 and then renouncing them all, how could they be saved? They have rejected and turned away from God's only plan of salvation. If a person were sick and refused the only kind of medicine which would bring healing, that person would have rejected the only method of getting well. If an individual were drowning and rejected the only rope thrown, he or she would be turning away from the only chance of being rescued. So it is with our salvation—there is one plan. Acts 4:12 makes this clear: "Salvation is found in no one else, for there is no other name under heaven given to men by which we must be saved."

"They are crucifying the Son of God all over again and subjecting him to public disgrace." Can you imagine crucifying our Lord all over again and subjecting Him to public disgrace? This person's act of apostasy is the same as crucifying our Savior again. The verse comes close to saying if you were at the cross the day Jesus was crucified, you would join with the crowd shouting, "Crucify Him, Crucify Him," and then be among those who were driving the nails through His hands and feet. How graphic is this person's rejection of Christ!

In a way this crime goes beyond the crime of those who actually crucified Christ because, as Jesus said from the cross, those people did not know what they were doing. In Hebrews 6, this person—with all his or her spiritual opportunity and insights—was holding Christ up publicly as deserving the horror of the cross. This included exhibiting Jesus to the passing multitude as if He ought to have this kind of suffering, rejection, and contempt.

A Warning to Christians

In two millenniums the church as a whole has not been able to make a decision on whether Hebrews 6 is referring to Christians or non-Christians. While I share in the struggle, all the things this person experienced in verses 4 and 5 lead me to lean toward the group who believe the text is speaking of Christians. I don't know how the things spoken of here—being enlightened, tasting the heavenly gift, sharing in the Holy Spirit, tasting the goodness of the Word of God, and the powers of the coming age—could be experienced by someone who had not come to Christ. Just one small insight is that some form of the word "enlightened" was often used in early Christian writings to refer to those coming to Christ.

If you were to ask me if I believe any Christian has ever done what Hebrews 6 is saying, I would quickly answer "No."

In verse 9 the writer says, "Even though we speak like this, dear friends, we are confident of better things in your case—things that accompany salvation." So, why this dreadful warning? The writer is letting us know apostasy is terrible. He is passionate about keeping believers from apostasy, which was rampant at that time in the unregenerate world.

Let's look at these verses another way. Could it be this experience of repentance and faith was not genuine? Perhaps. However, they had experienced magnificent things that Scripture seems to indicate are reserved for genuine Christians. This begs the question of how could one have these experiences without coming to salvation?

Check out 1 John 2:19. "They went out from us, but they did not really belong to us. For if they had belonged to us, they would have remained with us; but their going showed that none of them belonged to us." Significantly, this verse does not include a listing of experiences shared only by true believers such as are listed in Hebrews 6.

Why do you suppose the writer gives such stern warning to those who have experienced so much? I believe the severe statement was for the following reasons:

1. The writer of Hebrews wanted to keep genuine Christians from taking their faith lightly and living like unbelievers.

2. He wanted to tell Christians of all generations and nations how great is the sin of moving away from the things of Christ.

3. He wanted to guard us from any temptation towards apostasy.

It could be like saying a fall from a certain precipice would cause certain death—a statement meant to keep us from getting too close to the edge and falling.

4. He wanted Christians to understand the benefit and responsibility of being enlightened and the unreasonableness and punishment of leaving this privileged position.

5. He wanted them to seriously consider the privilege of tasting the heavenly gift (1 Peter 2:3 also uses this wording to speak of believers), what it means to have eternal salvation, forgiveness, enlightenment, the sanctifying influences of the Holy Spirit, and so much more. Think about it! Imagine sharing in the Holy Spirit and then losing that!

6. He wanted them to keep in mind the blessing of experiencing the goodness of the Word of God.

7. He wanted them to delight in the privilege of experiencing, while on earth, "the powers of the coming age."

8. And then, He wants them to consider the dire thought of verse 6: "if they fall away, to be brought back to repentance, because to their loss they are crucifying the Son of God all over again and subjecting him to public disgrace."

Here again the stakes are high! It is right that people consider these warnings. They are in Scripture for our benefit and for very specific purposes. On the other hand, it should encourage all believers that the means God has used to preserve His people from apostasy is adequate. There is no evidence one has ever fallen away to this extent after having experienced all that was listed in these verses. Verse 9 is an affirmation. Be encouraged that regardless of what you and I have done, God will not forsake us. "Those who know your name will trust in you, for you, Lord, have never forsaken those who seek you" (Psalm 9:10). Also of encouragement is John 10:27-28: "My sheep listen to my voice; I know them, and they follow me. I give them eternal life, and they shall never perish; no one can snatch them out of my hand." The Lord considers it His task to keep His people from apostasy and He will not fail.

The Blessing or Curse of God

Hebrews 6:7-8 contains an interesting and clarifying illustration intended to show the consequences of not making proper use of the privileges we have as Christians. It is like the earth. If it absorbs the rain and produces an abundant harvest, it is useful. If it does not absorb the rain and does not produce a good crop, it is useless. It is cursed if it does not take advantage of what it has received. Verse 7, "Land that drinks in the rain often falling on it and that produces a crop useful to those for whom it is farmed receives the blessing of God." This verse makes clear there is purpose to what God has given us. He plans on us becoming what His gifts allow us to become, and to use what His gifts empower us to do. This is the opposite of the apostasy spoken of earlier in verses 4-6. Then verse 8, "But land that produces thorns and thistles is worthless and is in danger of being cursed. In the end it will be burned." This land has also received rain but bears thorns and thistles and is considered by God to be worthless. It is abandoned and "in the end it will be burned."

We all have a choice. We can have the blessing of God or the curse of God. There is no question but there is a cost to verse 7. To take what God has given us and use it to grow spiritually goes contrary to many of our natural, selfish inclinations and desires. Further, to take the gifts God has given us and use them for others is magnanimous and contrary to the sinful world around us. It will cost us time, effort, and other resources. However, Jesus said in Matthew 10:38, "...anyone who does not take his cross and follow me is not worthy of me."

We have to decide. Is the blessing of God worth taking up our cross and following Him? Or, as verse 7 says, take what God gives us and produce a crop that is useful. Do we want to live for temporal or eternal values? The wise thing is to take responsibility for what God has given us and be useful to God and others. The difference of being self-centered or God-centered is like the difference of wasting or investing our lives if we are to think in terms of eternal values.

By the way, there is great joy in a life lived well, even though it is contrary to the basically selfish nature with which we were born. If we don't take responsibility for what He has given, we will receive His curse—verse 8 makes this clear. I want to stay an infinite distance from God's curse! A friend of mine said, "I ain't no whiz but what I is, is His." To not follow Him brings His curse, destruction, and a life without value that is ultimately overrun with fire. Whatever the end of verse 8 refers to, I want no part of it!

Let's stop the cycle and live for everlasting values. Let's look toward our real home where we will spend a life that never ends.

Paul, writing from prison said, "But our citizenship is in heaven. And we eagerly await a Savior from there, the Lord Jesus Christ, who, by the power that enables him to bring everything under his control, will transform our lowly bodies so that they will be like his glorious body" (Philippians 3:20-21). That surely beats being "worthless and…in danger of being cursed. In the end it will be burned."

So, we can pay the price of following and serving Christ in an unselfish and dedicated way and receive His blessing; or we can go on our self-centered way and receive the curse of God. I decided which price I want to pay—have you? It is like relationships with family and friends. We reap what we sow. If we are good friends, we will have good friends. If we treat our family members in loving ways, we will find love in our home. We choose. Most people are responders and if we pay the price of acting as we should, even when we don't feel like it, we will often receive similar treatment from others.

Be Holy in All You Do

We live in a generation and in a nation where it is popular to claim that you are a Christian—even a born again Christian. I take comfort that God alone is the judge. We need to remember it is more than praying a prayer and living as we please. Scripture says, "…be holy in all you do; for it is written: 'Be holy, because I am holy' " (1 Peter 1:15-16). Speaking of heaven, Revelation 21:27 says, "Nothing impure will ever enter it, nor will anyone who does what is shameful or deceitful, but only those whose names are written in the Lamb's book of life." Romans

1:24-27 speaks of people who lived an abhorrently sinful life to the extent that:

> ...God gave them over in the sinful desires of their hearts to sexual impurity for the degrading of their bodies with one another. They exchanged the truth of God for a lie, and worshiped and served created things rather than the Creator—who is forever praised. Amen. Because of this, God gave them over to shameful lusts. Even their women exchanged natural relations for unnatural ones. In the same way the men also abandoned natural relations with women and were inflamed with lust for one another. Men committed indecent acts with other men, and received in themselves the due penalty for their perversion.

A few verses later Romans 1:32 says, "...they not only continue to do these very things but also approve of those who practice them."

So, how serious is this kind of sin? 1 Corinthians 6:9-10, "Do you not know that the wicked will not inherit the kingdom of God? Do not be deceived: Neither the sexually immoral nor idolaters nor adulterers nor male prostitutes nor homosexual offenders...will inherit the kingdom of God." A clarifying word is appropriate here. I am not arguing for or against whether or not one is born with certain tendencies (homosexuality, arsonists, kleptomaniacs, etc.) but rather that the practice in living these things out and yielding to these urges is the issue. We are all tempted in certain and different ways. I was told recently of a Christian leader—a favorite author who never married—who had homosexual desires, but never acted upon them. In fact, I did not know he had homosexual tendencies until after his death. I consider him a godly model. "Being tempted is not sin, yielding to the temptation is sin," is a statement that bears remembering.

However, I have a deep concern because sometimes the church is more impacted by the sinful world than the sinful world is impacted by the church. As the culture spirals downward, the church holds a higher standard but often declines at the same rate—just 20 steps back. We are asked to be salt and light to the world, not caught up in its values and practices (Matthew 5:13-16).

I am a lover at heart, not a judge. God is both judge and jury. However, over decades of ministry, I have been concerned about those who profess to be believers but whose lives do not manifest the Holy Spirit indwelling them and, along with that, don't live out the fruit of the Spirit (Galatians 5:22-23). I hope all who read this book take seriously the chapter on "What If You Only Think You Are Going to Heaven?" If the road to heaven is narrow and most take the natural, wide road that leads to everlasting destruction, there is much room for concern. For those whose citizenship is in heaven (Philippians 3:20), there is to be a demonstration that they are Spirit-led people who are heading for an eternity with Him.

Confident of Better Things

Hebrews 6:9 offers much light and interesting insight. "Even though we speak like this, dear friends, we are confident of better things in your case—things that accompany salvation." The writer of Hebrews seemed confident they either were or would become strong believers in Christ. Why did the writer take us through this very difficult series of verses only to say in verse 9 that he is confident they had not done those things? Here are a couple of possibilities:

1. Though he was "confident of better things" for them, we don't know if he meant all of them or the majority. Perhaps his use of the word "confident" had an element of hope in it rather than knowing without doubt. However, the warning he gave is good for all of us.

2. It is all right to state a hypothetical case even though one is certain that event would never happen. For example, we could ponder what would happen if the ocean overflowed a continent or if the sun ceased to rise, and still be entirely certain such an event would never occur.

There is another disturbing passage in the book of Hebrews. As a child I read Hebrews 10:26-27 over and over again and concluded there was a good chance I had violated the warning. I also wondered if this sin was widespread among Christians. It says, "If we deliberately keep on sinning after we have received the knowledge of the truth, no sacrifice for sins is left, but only a fearful expectation of judgment and of raging fire that will consume the enemies of God." I was afraid I was guilty. I cannot imagine any believer who has "received the knowledge of the truth" who has not, at some time, deliberately sinned. If you have been anxious about this, there is help. Remember the words of 1 John 1:8: "If we claim to be without sin, we deceive ourselves and the truth is not in us." Sinning is universal among Christians and non-Christians.

Don't "Continue to Continue" to Sin

In Hebrews 10:26 it says: "If we *deliberately keep on* sinning…" (emphasis mine). Who is the writer talking about? Someone committing sin like all of us do? Or, is he talking about a pattern of sinning? When we put our faith in Christ we are "born again" (John 3:3, 7). In John 3 Jesus speaks of our fleshly birth and of our spiritual birth. When a baby is born, a new life has entered the world. When we receive Christ into our life, our natural life of flesh has also become a life with God. The Holy Spirit dwells within—Jesus refers to this as being born of the Spirit—"born again" (John 3:3). He also calls our body "a temple of the Holy Spirit, who is in you, whom you have received from God" (1 Corinthians 6:19). Our first birth was of the flesh and this second birth is of the Holy Spirit. This new life is indwelt and thus energized by the Holy Spirit.

Now things change—we still sin but we are not comfortable when "we deliberately keep on sinning." There are two parts. One is, we are continuing to continue to sin "after we have received the knowledge of the truth" and we have turned away from God's only plan of eternal salvation. This verse concludes with "no sacrifice for sins is left."

Let's look deeper at Hebrews 10:26 for clarity. What born again person would do this? When we have the Holy Spirit living within us, and we see eternal values as far exceeding temporal values, would we do this? Or, is the writer of Hebrews giving us fair warning in another effort to impress on us the importance and the assumption of holy living for those who are in Christ and Christ in them?

We are helped here by looking at 1 John 3:

Verse 6: "No one who lives in him keeps on sinning. No one who continues to sin has either seen him or known him."

Verse 9: "No one who is born of God will continue to sin, because God's seed remains in him; he cannot go on sinning, because he has been born of God."

The first is a person who "is born of God" and the second is about those who live "in him" and "God's seed remains in him" which is followed by "he cannot go on sinning." It is often suggested that the Greek language clarifies this passage since the verb used here for "sin" means to "continue to continue." This insight from the original Greek wording makes a clear case that continuing in sin is different from the time-to-time sin of the Christian. The person who continues to continue in their sin is more comfortable in their sin than is the true believer who has been "born of God" and "God's seed remains in him" (1 John 3:9).

Bible commentator Barclay also notes that there is a subtle difference in tenses that makes a large difference in meaning. John tells believers in 1 John 2:1 not to sin. That verb "sin" is in the aorist tense which indicates a particular and definite act. This means he is telling Christians not to commit individual acts of sin. That is good teaching and consistent with all of Scripture. However, in the same verse it states that if they do, "…we have one who speaks to the Father in our defense—Jesus Christ, the Righteous One" (1 John 2:1). In other words, we have Jesus as our defense attorney (and He never loses)! Barclay writes concerning 1 John 3:9: "On the other hand in both cases the verb 'to sin' is in the present tense, and indicates continuous, constant and habitual action" (William Barclay, *Letters of John and Jude*. The Westminster Press, 1960).

John is dealing with two sets of thinking here: those who believe they are perfect and without sin, and others who think it doesn't matter if they sin. Consequently he uses strong language to tell Christians to avoid sin. At the same time he gives balance here by stating in 1 John 1:8: "If we claim to be without sin, we deceive ourselves and the truth is not in us." One sin is inconsistent with the holiness of God and the aim (not the claim) of the Christian is not to sin. Think of the utter incongruity of a *life* of sin. Clarifying and ominous is the previously quoted 1 John 2:19: "They went out from us, but they did not really belong to us. For if they had belonged to us, they would have remained with us; but their going showed that none of them belonged to us."

New Creations

Let's go back to the book of Hebrews. Why such a harsh response to the sinning mentioned there? Because this person is deliberately continuing in their sin and has, in essence, turned away from the only means of forgiveness God has given. "If we deliberately keep on sinning after we have received the knowledge of the truth, no sacrifice for sins is left" (Hebrews 10:26). God is serious about His children living a holy life! He told us, "Be holy, because I am holy" (1 Peter 1:16). The verses in this chapter and throughout the Old and New Testaments make it clear that God expects His people to live a holy life.

For God to require a holy life is consistent with what He has done for and in us. We are made holy by Christ in two ways: first, He takes all our sins away (Psalm 103:12); and second, He gives us His righteousness (Romans 4:22-24). When we make an issue of sin and holiness, we are in synch with Scripture. We have been born of the Spirit. Jesus told Nicodemus (John 3:6) that "Flesh gives birth to flesh, but the Spirit gives birth to spirit." He was making clear something supernatural happens when we come to Christ. We become, according to 2 Corinthians 5:17, "...a new creation; the old has gone, the new has come!" 1 John 5:18 says, "We know that anyone born of God does not continue to sin; the one who was born of God keeps him safe, and the evil one cannot harm him."

There is a difference now. Though we sin, we don't want to wallow in our sin. We do not continue to continue. We keep short accounts with God. We don't feel comfortable in sin as we did before we became new creations. At the risk of being redundant, but at the same time deeply concerned that the issue in Hebrews 10:26-27 is understood, I add a comment. One who continues to continue in their sin has turned away from God's only provision for the forgiveness of sin. That's why there is "no sacrifice for sins left." There is only one way of having our sins forgiven and when we turn away from that one way, it isn't that God wouldn't forgive us; it is that we have decided to live in sin rather than take advantage of His forgiveness.

These verses in Hebrews are saying there is one means offered by God for forgiveness and salvation. It is through the sacrifice of the Lamb of God (Jesus) at Calvary. People heard about this and some accepted Christ. Others rejected Him and continued on without repentance and belief. Because there is no other available sacrifice for sin, what remains for them is stated in Hebrews 10:27: "…a fearful expectation of judgment and of raging fire that will consume the enemies of God."

This is frightening. Furthermore, it will be a terrifying thing for those who stand before God and He says: "Depart from me, you who are cursed, into the eternal fire prepared for the devil and his angels…Then they will go away to eternal punishment, but the righteous to eternal life" (Matthew 25:41, 46). How does this fit with verses we have previously used such as John 6:37, Romans 10:13, and Revelation 22:17? Remember that no verse in Scripture makes another verse untrue. Every verse has a path to the cross and every verse is consistent with all other verses. Each verse should be interpreted in the light of the entire Bible. Every verse is true. Every verse has its part in the whole of the message of God as He reveals Himself to us.

I am sorry for each sin I have committed. However, and not to belittle the seriousness of sinning—especially willfully sinning—I am delighted with the mercy of God. Rather than rejecting it as do those referred to in Hebrews 10:26, we need to embrace and trust in God's immeasurable love and mercy. First John 2:1-2 records these magnificent words,

My dear children, I write this to you so that you will not sin. But if anybody does sin, we have one who speaks to the Father in our defense—Jesus Christ, the Righteous One. He is the atoning sacrifice for our sins, and not only for ours but also for the sins of the whole world.

Jesus has paid the price. The next step is ours (See 2 Peter 1:3ff).

Living God's Way

There are other places in the Bible that speak of sin not forgiven. In every case, if the person would come to Christ in repentance and faith, he or she would be forgiven. We will look at two situations. Proverbs 29:1 says, "A man who remains stiff-necked after many rebukes will suddenly be destroyed—without remedy." Here God states the outcome of a person who is repeatedly rebuked and pays no heed; he "will suddenly be destroyed—without remedy." Many times I heard Billy Graham quote this verse in evangelistic campaigns. These people referred to in Proverbs 29:1 refused the rebukes and because of the path they chose, they were destroyed. One cannot take the wrong steps and end up in the right place. It does not mean everything will be the way we want. We live in a fallen world. 1 John 5:19 says, "...the whole world is under the control of the evil one." Our jobs will not always be perfect, nor will relationships. Our cars will break down, taxes will often be higher than we want, and there may be too much month at the end of the money! Reading and following Proverbs can keep us from going down the wrong moral and ethical paths. "Wise up!" is a theme that runs throughout Proverbs.

Before the Israelites entered the Promised Land, God told them through Moses:

> See, I have taught you decrees and laws as the Lord my God commanded me, so that you may follow them in the land you are entering to take possession of it. Observe them carefully, for this will show your wisdom and understanding to the nations, who will hear about all these decrees and say, "Surely this great nation is a wise and understanding people" (Deuteronomy 4:5-6).

More encouragement to walk in the ways of God comes from Psalm 19:7: "The law of the Lord is perfect, reviving the soul. The statutes of the Lord are trustworthy, making wise the simple." There is only one way to live…God's way. It is God who made us, it is God who made the world, and it is God who wrote the principles on how to live in the world. No wonder His way is the best way.

Proverbs 1:29-33 says:

> Since they hated knowledge and did not choose to fear the Lord, since they would not accept my advice and spurned my rebuke, they will eat the fruit of their ways and be filled with the fruit of their schemes. For the waywardness of the simple will kill them, and the complacency of fools will destroy them; but whoever listens to me will live in safety and be at ease, without fear of harm.

Proverbs 10:25 provides a contrast: "When the storm has swept by, the wicked are gone, but the righteous stand firm forever." Proverbs 28:18 confirms this: "He whose walk is blameless is kept safe, but he whose ways are perverse will suddenly fall."

These verses and many others tell us that God has set up a plan for us to follow and it is only His plan that works well. The primary verse we looked at, Proverbs 29:1, concludes with the death of the person. That is why there is no longer a remedy. If he or she were still alive, he or she could come to the Lord in repentance and faith, follow His ways, and enjoy a good life on earth with the bright prospect of heaven.

The other situation is mentioned in 1 John 5:16-17:

> If anyone sees his brother commit a sin that does not lead to death, he should pray and God will give him life. I refer to those whose sin does not lead to death. There is a sin that leads to death. I am not saying that he should pray about that. All wrongdoing is sin, and there is a sin that does not lead to death.

John is speaking of a particular sin that brings death, apparently at a specific time. He is telling us there are times when a Christian (he calls this person "a brother") sins so seriously that God apparently decides things would be better off with that person dead rather than alive. No one seems to know how to thoroughly explain what the sin is that leads to death, why it is so serious, nor the varied ways of death because of it. Most likely there is not a particular sin in view here but rather an apostasy, the denial of Christ, and the abandonment or rejection of faith in Christ. Some link this to Hebrews 6:4-6 and Hebrews 10:26ff. Others link it to the unpardonable sin in Matthew 12, Mark 3, and Luke 12. In any event, none of these verses exclude a person from salvation who wants to come to Christ in repentance and faith.

Acts 5:1-10 brings Ananias and Sapphira to center stage as an illustration. I agree with Earl Palmer in *The Preacher's Commentary* when he quotes F. F. Bruce suggesting this text may be best interpreted in its most literal sense: "I suggest that it is quite literally a sin which has death as its consequence. What John is doing, in that case, is to make it plain that he does not advocate praying for the dead" (F. F. Bruce, *Answers to Questions*. Zondervan, 1972). God may not punish by immediate death. Some sins have a rapid consequence of death and some sins do not. We know all sin ultimately leads to death. Like Adam and Eve, we have all sinned and at some point we will die. Here, however, he is talking about sins that have death as a direct consequence. First Corinthians 3:17 and 1 Corinthians 11:30 are other verses that connect death and sin.

All of this causes us to ask, "How do we know what the sin is that leads to death and sin that does not, so we know how to pray?" Actually, we don't know. What we do know is that God is God and does what is best. At the very least, God is making a stern warning through these verses. We must recognize God is not to be taken lightly. Our relationship with Him should be front and center in our lives. When we come to Christ we are made new creations and it will change the way we live. We do not continue in our sins. We are uncomfortable in the ways of a sinful world—we don't want to "continue to continue."

Taking this to a logical conclusion, if we help a Christian who is grievously sinning, we may be part of prolonging his or her life. James 5:20 alludes to this as does Proverbs 10:27, 11:19,

13:14, and 19:16. Our prayers have a great impact. Yet, God is God and while we may pray another way, He exercises His freedom, omnipotence, and omniscience, and does as He sees best.

Can You Sin So Much
You Cannot Come to Christ?

We all have an Achilles Heel—a vulnerable spot that Satan knows and targets. He is smart. First he tempts us and if we yield to temptation and sin, we must then go to the Lord confessing the sin. Satan often comes back after we are forgiven and accuses us of the sin he tempted us to commit. Graciously, God remembers our sin no more. Satan remembers and often makes sure we do as well.

Some people believe there is a certain sin they committed that God will not forgive. Though they believe God forgives their other sins, they are afraid this one goes beyond His forgiveness. The Bible assures us God will forgive if we come to Him in repentance and faith.

Let me be clear, however, God hates sin. He has given us the ability to resist temptation (1 Corinthians 10:13). It grieves God when we sin. He takes it seriously. Can you imagine sending your only son from heaven to earth to be crucified, ridiculed, spit upon, and to die for people who you knew would reject him? While that gives us insight into how much God detests sin, it also gives us a glimpse into how much He loves us.

In Hebrews 6 and Hebrews 10 we looked at verses showing the seriousness of sin. We must not treat sin lightly. First John 2:19 shows a dividing line. While we are neither judge nor jury, this verse gives us insight into what could be troubling to us when we see people who have insincerely "prayed the prayer" or made a false profession when it says, "They went out from us, but they did not really belong to us. For if they had belonged to us, they would have remained with us; but their going showed that none of them belonged to us" (1 John 2:19). I remember reading, "Continuance is the test of reality."

There are two extremes among Christians: 1) some believe they have come to the place where they never sin (though 1 John 1:8 says, "If we claim to be without sin, we deceive ourselves and the truth is not in us") and 2) some believe it really doesn't matter much if we sin because God will forgive us. This latter issue reminds me of what Paul said to the Romans: "What shall we say, then? Shall we go on sinning so that grace may increase? By no means!" (Romans 6:1-2).

There is no one in the entire world that has sinned to the extent that if they come to Christ in repentance and faith, they will be turned away. A high water mark in Scripture is John 6:37 telling us that anyone who comes to Christ will not be turned away. *In faith. 2/23/19*

Personal Reflection or Discussion Questions

1. How do we know if we can be forgiven of all our sins?

2. How holy do we need to be? Is there a litmus test?

3. Aside from the seriousness of the passages in Hebrews and 1 John, why is "holiness" such a big issue?

4. Who comes to your mind when you ask, "Who is the holiest person I know?" Why?

5. What is the ultimate way we gain assurance that we have not committed the sins spoken of in Hebrews and/or 1 John?

Chapter 7

Can You Lose Your Salvation?

John 10:28-29

My first pastorate was a little Baptist church in southern California where expressions like "eternal security" and "once saved always saved" were common. I also heard critics of this position say, "People who believe this way think a person can accept the Lord and then live as they please." People tend to have entrenched views on this topic, many ready with supporting Bible verses with which to argue their point. I'm not surprised at the differing views, but I am somewhat taken back by the prominence some give this issue.

One Sunday, while teaching the adult class at that little church, I asked how many believed in eternal security (also called "eternal salvation" and "perseverance of the saints"). Half the hands went up. I had thought most, if not all, would raise their hands. So I asked, "How many do not believe in eternal security?" The other half raised their hands. Some consider this debate a problem. Both sides can support their position with Scripture. The most helpful illustration I know was given to me by my Uncle Jasper, Marilyn Meberg's dad (See Preface), who was a thoughtful, gifted pastor. The illustration goes like this: Let's suppose one Sunday the town drunk went to a church that believed a person can lose their salvation. He prayed to invite Christ into his life. A couple years later, after being faithful to Christ and his church, he again became the town drunk. That church would say he probably became a Christian but lost his salvation. Consequently, he needed to be saved. Now, let's say that town drunk went to a church one Sunday that believed Christians can't lose their salvation. He prayed to receive Christ into his life. A couple years later, after being faithful to Christ and his church, he again became the town drunk. That church would say he never really received salvation. He prayed the prayer but wasn't sincere; so he never was part of the family of God. Consequently, he needed to be saved. In either situation, the end result is the same. This person needs to come to Christ in repentance and faith and receive salvation. This illustration impacted my view of this subject and placed the issue in a different light.

This illustration, along with the fact that there are many godly, biblical theologians on both sides, should give us pause before we make this an earth-shaking issue! This is not to say it is unimportant—we are not using a cannon to shoot a bird. It does, however, call for study and grace. It makes good discussion, but in the course of discussion, it should not be divisive. Is it safe to say if one sincerely accepts Christ as Savior and Lord and lives a Christian life, he or she doesn't need to worry about losing his or her salvation? Is it safe to say if a person has made a profession of faith but there is no evidence of a changed life, that person needs to come to Christ in repentance and faith for salvation? I remember hearing my dad, who believed in eternal security, say more than once, "Regardless of the prayer you prayed, you can't live like the devil and go to heaven when you die."

How Long Is Eternal Life?

Let's look at both positions. I believe in eternal salvation (I like this term better than "eternal security" though I intend the same meaning). Jesus promises eternal life to those who believe in Him. How long is eternal life? It is eternal. Our new life in Christ doesn't just last until we sin again. It begins at conversion and because it is "eternal life," it extends throughout eternity. A favorite verse, John 3:16, says we receive eternal life. There are many verses supporting the eternality of our salvation. Note: John 6:39-40, 10:28-29; 1 Peter 1:4; Ephesians 1:13 and 4:30.

I don't see biblical support for believing that you can have eternal life one moment and not have it at another. There is no parenthetical statement after a promise of eternal life that says, "unless you sin again." At the same time, we must realize there are verses that seem to make our eternal security conditional. One of these is Hebrews 3:6: "But Christ is faithful as a son over God's house. And we are his house, if we hold on to our courage and the hope of which we boast." How can we reconcile an eternal salvation and the "if" of Hebrews 3:6? I believe the issue

is if a person has been born of the Spirit and becomes a new
creature in Christ, he or she will hold on to courage and hope.
Not only will born again people hold on to their courage and
hope, but God holds on to them. God is involved in keeping us
in His family. First Corinthians 1:8-9 says, "He will keep you
strong to the end, so that you will be blameless on the day of our
Lord Jesus Christ. God, who has called you into fellowship with
his Son Jesus Christ our Lord, is faithful."

A good friend of mine, a Christian leader, when writing about
the issue of being assured we would end up in heaven, went to
a passage of Scripture that settled this for him. He referred me
to John 10:28-29 where Jesus said, "I give them eternal life, and
they shall never perish; no one can snatch them out of my hand.
My Father, who has given them to me, is greater than all; no
one can snatch them out of my Father's hand." My friend said,
"I will always remember the power of John 10:28-29 in my own
heart and spirit. The security of being held by Jesus in His hand
and then to have the Father place His hand around the hand
of Jesus—this picture of being held secure in an overlapping
and double-hand clasp by God the Son and God the Father—
gripped my heart and mind in ways that have never left me."

New Creation Means Changed Lives

In salvation an amazing and powerful thing happens to us.
We are born of the Spirit just as we had previously been born of
the flesh. This new life changes us to the extent that we are called
a new creation. This is a miraculous experience and of eternal
significance. We are now united with Christ. Second Corinthians

5:17 says, "If anyone is in Christ, he is a new creation; the old has gone, the new has come!" This is no small thing. This is life changing—we are new creations! The old has gone and the new has come. We are now sons and daughters of God, part of His family. We have been given eternal life. We are held secure in that overlapping and double-hand clasp.

Some believers, as mentioned earlier, are concerned that a confidence in eternal security leads to the belief that a person can accept Christ and then return to his or her old ways of living for sin, self, and the devil. However, if this miraculous spiritual birth has taken place, this person would not want to live that way. It would be an uncomfortable lifestyle. According to 1 Corinthians 6:19, God the Holy Spirit makes our body His temple. With God living in us, we don't even want to live in ungodly ways for long. This is why Augustine could rightly say, "Love God and do as you please."

Further, there is a logical challenge to the idea of losing salvation because of sin. It is this: How many sins does it take to lose one's salvation? Is it one, ten, or could it be a hundred? Or, are there certain sins that take salvation away? Is there a list of sins that will take our salvation away and another list of sins that won't? Let me quickly add, however, regardless of how I began this paragraph, I do not allow logic to determine what I believe. I believe whatever the Bible says, whether it fits human logic or not. Think how insignificant, puny, and stunted our logic is compared to the infinite wisdom and knowledge of God. Isaiah 55:8-9 sheds light on this infinite gap: " 'For my thoughts are not your thoughts, neither are your ways my ways,' declares the Lord. 'As the heavens are higher than the earth, so are my ways higher than your ways and my thoughts than your thoughts.' "

An answer to the sincere concern of those who believe Christians can lose their salvation is that when we are born of the Spirit and, as a consequence, now have the Holy Spirit residing in our bodies, we do not want to live the way we used to live. Furthermore, heaven is our real home. We already have citizenship there (Philippians 3:20). We do sin but with the Holy Spirit living within us, and a realization of heaven being our eternal home, we have a new power, new affections, new hopes, new goals and a new citizenship. Add to this that high water mark verse in Psalm 37:4: "Delight yourself in the Lord and he will give you the desires of your heart." That's living at its best!

Beyond these things, Romans 8:1 gives a remarkable promise: "There is now no condemnation to those who are in Christ Jesus." Can you imagine anything with the profundity, depth, fullness, assurance, guarantee, significance, extensiveness, and comprehensiveness of Romans 8:1? Think of how complete God's promise of sin removal and condemnation acquittal is in the last words of Christ from the cross, "It is finished" (John 19:30). Redemption is complete. The price has been paid—condemnation is gone! Our sin has been forgiven. Would anyone want to step out of a life like this?

I struggle deeply when I see people who served Christ for many years with love and fervency and then leave that life and enter apostasy, never to return to fellowship with Christ. Are they in the Hebrews 6:4-8 and Hebrews 10:26-27 company? What happened? What do we not see about their life and previous experiences?

So then a good exhortation for all of us, regardless of what our belief is regarding whether or not one can lose their salvation, is in 1 John 2:28: "And now, dear children, continue in him, so that when he appears we may be confident and unashamed before him at his coming." The writer tells us to, "continue in him" so that when Jesus returns, "we may be confident and unashamed." Continue! The same author wrote that word seven times in the book of those who overcome (Revelation). He states these are the ones who will receive the eternal blessings.

Persevere in Doing the Will of God

What about those described in Matthew 7:21-23?

Not everyone who says to me, "Lord, Lord," will enter the kingdom of heaven, but only he who does the will of my Father who is in heaven. Many will say to me on that day, "Lord, Lord, did we not prophesy in your name, and in your name drive out demons and perform many miracles?" Then I will tell them plainly, "I never knew you. Away from me, you evildoers!"

There are many verses which remind us of Matthew 7:13-14: "Enter through the narrow gate. For wide is the gate and broad is the road that leads to destruction, and many enter through it. But small is the gate and narrow the road that leads to life, and only a few find it." Keep this in mind and, at the same time, keep in mind it is an eternal salvation we are given. God holds on to us as we, with tenacity and through His strength, follow Christ in the world...this world which is under the control of Satan (1 John 5:19).

Incomplete !

Kept in His Hand

In light of all this, can we know we are going to heaven? Yes! How do we know? He has told us we can know (1 John 5:13). Look closely and celebrate that those who have been born of the Spirit are kept by God in His good hands. "I give them eternal life, and they shall never perish; no one can snatch them out of my hand. My Father, who has given them to me, is greater than all; no one can snatch them out of my Father's hand" (John 10:28-29). We may feel weak and vulnerable, but Christ is strong. He not only prays for us (Romans 8:34 and Hebrews 7:25) but Paul said in 1 Corinthians 1:8: "He [Jesus] will keep you strong to the end, so that you will be blameless on the day of our Lord Jesus Christ." We can say with Paul: "The Lord will rescue me from every evil attack and will bring me safely to his heavenly kingdom" (2 Timothy 4:18).

I look at Scripture and seek to understand the many facets of our eternal salvation. I am well aware that, "Now we see but a poor reflection as in a mirror" (1 Corinthians 13:12), and that "The secret things belong to the Lord our God" (Deuteronomy 29:29). With all of that as part of my understanding, I believe when a person genuinely and sincerely comes to Christ in repentance and faith, they receive eternal life and, because it is eternal life, they will never lose it. At the same time, I have high respect for those godly people who take a different view. I will love being with them in heaven and I love being with them now. None of us have a corner on interpreting these issues that have godly Christian scholarship supporting both opinions.

Summary of Chapter 7

Can You Lose Your Salvation?

This question is another one that has been debated over the centuries and unfortunately at times been divisive. Scripture makes clear that heaven is not for those living a continually sinful life regardless of what they are trusting in and regardless of what prayer was prayed. Scripture speaks of God having His children in His hands, promising that no one will be able to pluck them out. However, it is also clear that a truly converted person, born of the Spirit, doesn't want to live a continually sinful life.

It is confusing to reconcile God's clear standard that His people live a godly life, with those who profess to have accepted Christ but live like the unconverted. Pollster George Barna's research shows that the behavior of many professing Christians is indistinguishable from non-Christians. While the book of Revelation speaks of those who have overcome, 1 John stresses that continuing in the faith is the test of faith's reality.

Our logic cannot drive our theology. It is the Bible itself that tells us what is true. However, even with this understanding, there are verses used by people who believe one can lose their salvation and other verses that indicate a person who is saved is saved for all eternity.

I have even heard the argument that because we never lose our free will, we can choose to be "unsaved" as well as to be "saved." While the word "will" is in the Bible, the phrase "free will" is not, as related to salvation. This raises the issue, a major one for many, of how free our will is. Can "eternal" life be interrupted and made a temporary life because we sin or change our mind? It seems implausible to me that a person can enjoy the life of a Christian and then desire to turn away. I think of Hebrews 6:9 where, after speaking of people leaving the good things of God, the writer said he was sure it wasn't true of them but rather he believed they were living out "things that accompany salvation." What we have experienced is not just the results of a self-help program but rather it is the real, lasting, eternal life of being born again by the Spirit of God.

Can you lose your salvation? If you have a personal relationship with Christ and you live according to biblical standards, whichever position you hold, you don't need to worry about it. In any event, in your discussion and perhaps disagreement over this issue, do not bring disharmony to your church (Romans 12:18).

Personal Reflection or Discussion Questions

1. What are the two views of eternal security? What is your view of these two positions? Why?

2. What is the real driving force of a person who "prays the prayer" but does not continue in the faith?

3. What is God's role in keeping us in the faith?

4. What is our role in staying in the faith?

5. What are the primary things you and I should be doing to stay in the faith, and/or to live a life consistent with our faith?

6. Do you have loved ones whom you are sure have genuinely accepted Christ and yet are living for themselves and this present world? What do you consider your role in their lives while they live this way?

7. Does this chapter make you fear or take comfort in the reality of assurance of salvation? Why?

Chapter 8

Are Feelings Part of Assurance?
Romans 8:14-16
John 15:11, 16:24, 17:13

Feelings Change, Faith Doesn't

For many Christians, emotions can be a hindrance to assurance of salvation. They were for me. Are there new feelings that accompany salvation? Yes, but in my experience the feelings were different than I expected. When I didn't feel what I thought I ought to feel, I was afraid I wasn't a Christian. Has that been your experience? I pray that this chapter will be a turning point in assurance of salvation for all who want to know for certain they are going to heaven. I will explain the route God led me through to get out of the "feelings" rut I was in for several years.

...because those who are led by the Spirit of God are sons of God. For you did not receive a spirit that makes you a slave again to fear, but you received the Spirit of sonship. And by him we cry, "*Abba*, Father." The Spirit himself testifies with our spirit that we are God's children (Romans 8:14-16).

This verse used to confuse and trouble me: "The Spirit himself testifies with our spirit that we are God's children." I wondered how this testifying worked? Perhaps it wasn't a feeling, but was something I was to be aware of, though I didn't know what this "something" was. How would I know the Holy Spirit was testifying with my spirit? What did that feel like or what were the indications it was happening? I read William Newell's commentary on Romans. It has the finest illustration of this part of Scripture I have found. I want to pass it on—old language and old Bible translation—just the way I read it:

God, in this passage in Romans, does not address Himself at all to human intellect, but to the consciousness of His saints.

Much unnecessary and unfruitful questioning as to what is the witness of the Spirit has arisen. It is plain both in this passage (verses 15, 16) and from the great verse in Galatians 4:6: "Because ye are sons, God sent forth the *Spirit of His Son* into our hearts, crying, '*Abba*, Father,'" that the witness of the Spirit is the producing of the consciousness of being born of God, of belonging to His family, in Christ. And for us today who are in Christ, there should be the consciousness, not merely of babes, but of adult-sons. "God sent forth the Spirit of His Son into our hearts, crying, '*Abba*, Father.' " It is a sense of the very relation to the Father which Christ Himself has as Son! Mark, in this we do not "know" the Son, for He is the second person of the Deity; but we do know the Father, and the Son "willeth to reveal Him" by sending the blessed Spirit for that purpose (See Matthew 11:27). How beautifully sweet is the recognition of its parents by a babe, a child! Unconscious, instinctive, yet how real!

Now the witness of the Spirit is to the fact of our relationship. How foolish it would be, and how sad, if a child should fall into the delusion that it must have certain "feelings" if it is to believe itself a child of its parents. The unconscious certainty of the relationship is the beauty of it. There are, indeed, certain tests Divinely given us, by which to assure ourselves. Most of these, perhaps, are in the great Epistle of Fellowship, First John, "fellowship with the Father and with His Son, Jesus Christ." "I have written unto you, little children, because ye know the Father (2:13). Beloved now we are children of God, and it is not yet made manifest what we shall be. We know that, if He shall be manifested, we shall be like Him for we shall see Him even as He is (3:2). Hereby we know that He abideth in us, by the Spirit which He gave us" (3:24).

Newell continues:

"The Spirit Himself beareth witness with our spirit." "With our spirit"—We are not told that the Spirit bears witness

to our spirit, as if the knowledge that we are God's children were some unheard of, undreamed matter to our own spirits. But He *beareth witness with our spirit*, showing that the child of God, having had communicated to him God's own nature (2 Peter 1:4), Christ's own life (1 Corinthians 6:17), is fundamentally, necessarily conscious of the glorious fact of filial relationship to God. Along with this consciousness, the Spirit indwelling witnesses, enabling us, moving us, to cry, "*Abba*, Father." There is life before this, just as the new-born babe has life and breath before it forms a syllable. It is significant that the Spirit indwelling is the power whereby we cry, "*Abba*, Father,"—by His enlightenment, His encouragement, His energy.

good ?

The operations of a man's mind either in philosophy or in science constitute an eternal quest for certainty. The conclusions of philosophy are based upon theories and hypotheses, and are always being challenged and perpetually overthrown by succeeding new schemes of philosophy. And even the dearest discoveries of science await new explanations—of the very constitution of the Universe they are invented in.

But with the child of God—the born-again family, there is no such uncertainty! A child of God *knows*. And the blessed Holy Spirit, by whose inscrutable power he was born again, keeps forever witnessing with his consciousness,—and that through no processes of his mind, but directly, that he is a born-one of God.

This is most natural and could not be otherwise. Children in an earthly family grow up together as a family, their parents addressing them as children, their brothers and sisters knowing them to be such. It is the most beautiful thing in the natural world!

How much more certain, yea, how much more wonderful and beautiful, is the constantly witnessed relationship of His children to God: *the Spirit Himself beareth witness with our spirit, that we are born-ones of God.* Believers will find themselves calling God *Father* in their prayers and communion. This witness will spring up of itself in the heart that has truly rested in Christ and His shed blood. (William Newell, *Newell on Romans Verse by Verse.* Revised Edition. Moody Press, 1938)

In the course of writing this chapter, I have been "high on joy." I hope you are, too, but be aware that our responses are affected by our personality type. For example, a stoic person will probably demonstrate and "feel" things differently than an emotional person.

Further, the Romans 8:14-16 passage used in this chapter is not a "going to Disneyland joy." It is far deeper and comes with more meaning. However, these verses used to bother me as I will note later in this chapter. The following is an illustration of this kind of joy; the joy of belonging, not unlike belonging to a family on earth except we multiply it many times over because it is God's eternal family.

In a sermon, I once heard my dad tell the story of when he was in a terrible train wreck. The train suddenly and violently shook and jerked—there was the sound of metal against metal. Without thinking, Dad, knowing his life was in danger, called out, "Father." He didn't have to think about it. He didn't try to

analyze theologically whether or not it was appropriate to call on
His heavenly Father. He was in the family of God. He had "the
Spirit of sonship." Children of God come by this Spirit naturally.
"And by him we cry, '*Abba*, Father.' " "*Abba*" is a term of familial
love, like "daddy." A person who sincerely applies this term to
God has the spirit of a Christian. Note Romans 8:16: "The Spirit
himself testifies with our spirit that we are God's children." This
sense of son and daughtership is in our heart of hearts, whether
we are sad or happy, exhilarated or afraid.

The Spirit gives us a sense of family—an underlying consciousness that you and I are in God's family, not in Satan's family. I don't remember when this became real to me but I now
have a strong sense of being part of God's family. Some of you
who have received Christ (John 1:12) may be realizing now, for
the first time, you also have this sense of family and it gives you
a new level of assurance of salvation. Let's take the illustration
further. My children have a "sense" of being in our family. There
was never a time when I sat down with them and said, "I want
you to be aware that you are in our family." They had a deep-
seated sense of being part of our family—none of us questioned
it, we just knew. I know I am in God's family because the Holy
Spirit bears witness with my spirit that this is true.

Strange as it may seem, my struggle with what Christians
"ought" to feel started in church services. Listening to testimonies, I heard people say something like, "I accepted Christ as my
Savior 40 years ago and I've been happy ever since." This was a
problem to me! I had accepted Christ a few years before and I
wasn't always happy. Sometimes I was sad. Their testimony of
constant happiness caused me to doubt I was a Christian. Since
childhood, something in me desired a constant, joyful, inward

confirmation of my salvation. I believed joy was an entitlement of the salvation experience. Because I didn't understand how feelings of being a Christian demonstrated themselves, I questioned the validity of my salvation.

Where did my incorrect thinking come from? Not from the Bible—it came from the way I perceived the testimonies. If these people were happy all the time, why wasn't I? I was afraid the difference must be in the lack of my salvation experience because in their testimonies these believers tied their joy to their acceptance of Christ.

Without question, there are feelings associated with salvation. For example, when we think of some of the great facts of our salvation, including sins forgiven and the promise of eternity spent with God in heaven, how can they not bring us a certain kind of joy? The Swedish hymn writer, Carl Gustaf Boberg, appropriately expressed a kind of godly joy:

And when I think of God, His Son not sparing,
Sent Him to die, I scarce can take it in,
That on the cross, my burden gladly bearing,
He bled and died to take away my sin.

When Christ shall come with shout of acclamation
And take me home, what joy shall fill my heart!
Then I shall bow in humble adoration,
And there proclaim, My God, how great Thou art.

Chorus: Then sings my soul, my Savior God, to Thee;
How great Thou art, how great Thou art!

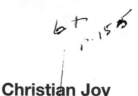

Christian Joy

In Chapters 15, 16, and 17 in the Gospel of John, Jesus speaks of the joy He intends for us. He even uses the phrase of "giving us his joy." We use the words "joy" and "happy" to describe a variety of things, from a spiritual experience to a trip to Disneyland. And then there are difficult life situations, neither spiritual nor non-spiritual, which we respond to with feelings that are opposite of joy. Think of the feelings from clinical depression or losing a loved one in death. On the other hand, think of the joy of catching a record-breaking fish, shooting a hole-in-one, or hearing an enthusiastic "yes" to a proposal for marriage.

God has given us other assurances, such as in 1 John 5:13: "I write these things to you who believe in the name of the Son of God so that you may know that you have eternal life." I have used this verse frequently because of the over-arching promise that we can know, and this verse resolutely gives affirmation. Our primary assurance that we are in the family of God comes by the witness of the Holy Spirit. There are more:

Have you sincerely called and asked for salvation?
(Romans 10:13)

Did you desire to come to Christ and, on that basis, come?
(Revelation 22:17)

Have you come to Christ? If you have, He has promised, "…whoever comes to me I will never drive away."
(John 6:37)

Have you confessed Christ verbally and do you believe
in your heart that God the Father has raised Him from
the dead?
(Romans 10:9)

Are you trusting in Christ, even if your faith is small?
(Acts 16:31)

These assurances are real reasons for joy. They don't necessarily generate emotional highs. I remember winning an election—that was an emotional high. A church Dee and I served gave us a cruise—that was an emotional high. Another church made me senior pastor emeritus and the gift of any trip we wanted to take—that gave us an emotional high.

Contrary to those feelings, I remember a friend's proposal experience. He told several friends when and how he would propose, creating an unusually romantic and clever setting. All were certain the woman would accept. All went well until the final step—presenting the beautiful ring. Upon seeing it, she said a devastatingly simple, "No." There was no rejoicing in that moment for my friend. Happiness continued at a low ebb the next day when he had to let his friends know her answer.

I was sad beyond words at the funeral of my mother and later my dad. So much was lost from my life. I knew they were with the Lord but they were gone from my fellowship. I loved them and I needed them. Though I was an adult and had been in ministry many years, they were still my chief advisors. And I had them all my life. I couldn't imagine life without them. In my limited understanding, while I trusted God, it seemed so wrong. Many, who were older and seemed to be contributing very little to life, still had good health. And now, life was over for my parents. We lowered their mortal bodies into the ground knowing we would not see them again in this life. I was happy for them but sad for myself, other family members, and a host of dear friends.

Now, where is the joy of the Lord in this? Underneath all my shattered emotions and feelings of loss, it was there. When I thought of my future first day in heaven, I had joy. There were several emotions going on at the same time: joy for them and their end to suffering, and then joy that we would someday be together again—this time forever with no sickness, pain, or death. No sin. No sadness. These opposing and parallel emotions were there, true and real. I think of the Southern Gospel song, "The First Day in Heaven." Just think what that day will be like. Mother and Dad over there with Jesus and, oh yes—there's Moses. "Hi, Paul. Hi, Adam. Hi, Grandpa"!

I want to point out that there is a wide range in people's feelings, all the way from their initial response when they place their faith in Christ to times like I have just described. We are all wired differently—that can be apparent at our initial point of faith as well as our ongoing life of faith. I remember leading a man to Christ who had been living a life of sin. He seemed to have no interest in knowing Christ. One day I decided to ask this stoic man if he would like to invite Christ into his life. Surprisingly, he said, "Yes." I invited him to come to my office where we could be alone. I prayed and he prayed after me. He expressed no emotion. I left my office believing nothing spiritual had happened. There was absolutely no indication of joy, optimism, excitement, or gratitude—emotions often displayed by a person when they place their faith in Christ. As the weeks grew into months and years, he grew into an all-out servant of Christ. He became chairman of the board of our church and remained strong and faithful, even during difficult times in that church. He and his wife, also a new Christian, were among the pillars of that church.

I remember my mother explaining a related issue. We were speaking of a delightful lady in our church who was always rejoicing. Her love for Christ "oozed out" of her like no one I knew. Mother explained: "Some people are made like this." As a junior high boy, I knew I didn't have feelings like this woman, whom I knew well. She inspired me and many others. It also bothered me that I didn't have the feelings that she had.

It is more than enough to be kept out of hell and able to enjoy heaven for all eternity. But Jesus goes on to tell us He will give us joy while on earth. He ended John 15:11 with: "…that your joy may be complete." Clearly He wasn't speaking of emotional ecstasy all the time. He even wept (John 11:35). Jesus is telling us we don't have to barely make it through life; we can have an extraordinary life.

While we won't always have an emotional high in our Christian life, certainly our feelings are involved. When we realize: our sins are forgiven, we are saved for eternity, we will be in a place where Jesus is the light and there is no sin, we will live in perfect, celestial bodies with no relational problems or family issues, and that every day will be a perfect day, how can we not at least be glad? In just three chapters of John, Jesus promised joy six times. Among them:

> "I have told you this so that my joy may be in you and that your joy may be complete" (John 15:11).

"Until now you have not asked for anything in my name. Ask and you will receive, and your joy will be complete" (John 16:24).

"I am coming to you now, but I say these things while I am still in the world, so that they may have the full measure of my joy within them" (John 17:13).

Considering the word "joy" as Jesus used it, I think of some of the distinguished people of Scripture who went through difficult times, such as Paul who speaks here from 1 Corinthians 4:9-13:

For it seems to me that God has put us apostles on display at the end of the procession, like men condemned to die in the arena. We have been made a spectacle to the whole universe, to angels as well as to men. We are fools for Christ, but you are so wise in Christ! We are weak, but you are strong! You are honored, we are dishonored! To this very hour we go hungry and thirsty, we are in rags, we are brutally treated, we are homeless. We work hard with our own hands. When we are cursed, we bless; when we are persecuted, we endure it; when we are slandered, we answer kindly. Up to this moment we have become the scum of the earth, the refuse of the world.

Would the word "happy," as usually defined, fit into Paul's situation? Other examples of this are Elijah in 1 Kings 18-19 and the Psalms of grief such as Psalm 25, 39, 51, 86, 102, and 120.

Prescription for Joy

In John 15:11, Jesus said, "I have told you this so that my joy may be in you and that your joy may be complete." Think of that—"my joy," Jesus said. What high quality joy! He has made provision for His joy to be "in you." This verse concludes with, "that your joy may be complete." Where else can you find a credible promise of obtaining complete joy that comes from God?

If it is His joy, it must come on His terms. We have His joy by living His way. Pointing us in the way of joy is 1 Thessalonians 5:16-18. We are encouraged to, "Be joyful always; pray continually; give thanks in all circumstances, for this is God's will for you in Christ Jesus." In addition, our lifestyle, when lived in the Spirit, will produce the fruit of the Spirit which is, "love, joy, peace, patience, kindness, goodness, faithfulness, gentleness and self-control" (Galatians 5:22-23). Fruit doesn't make an effort to become fruit. It is a result of a healthy tree or bush. It is a consequence. Think of how many people benefit, including yourself, when your life shows forth the fruit of the Spirit.

We see more of God's way being the best way of living in John 15:9-10 where Jesus made a remarkable statement giving the prescription for love: "As the Father has loved me, so have I loved you. Now remain in my love. If you obey my commands, you will remain in my love, just as I have obeyed my Father's commands and remain in his love." What was the requirement? Keeping His commands. What was a result? "...that your joy may be complete" (John 15:11). How's this for a new way of getting joy? So often God's approach is 180 degrees different than the sinful world's way.

Thoughts and values are related to joy. Colossians 3:1-4 says,

Since, then, you have been raised with Christ, set your
hearts on things above, where Christ is seated at the
right hand of God. Set your minds on things above, not
on earthly things. For you died, and your life is now hidden with Christ in God. When Christ, who is your life,
appears, then you also will appear with him in glory.

These verses lay out what we think about, what we care
about, and the way we view the basis of our life. And then the
phrase, "Christ, who is your life...," while it is moving to another point, makes us pause and think about Christ being our life.
How similar is this to Jesus being the vine and we the branches?
He makes a clear point that we should remain in Him and He in
us because, "No branch can bear fruit by itself; it must remain
in the vine. Neither can you bear fruit unless you remain in me"
(John 15:4). Is "fruit" the "fruit of the Spirit" or is it living a
productive life for God? Some think one thing, some think the
other. In either or both cases, they are attributes related to genuine joy.

In Christ's high priestly prayer of John 17, He prays to His
Father in heaven: "I am coming to you now, but I say these things
while I am still in the world, so that they may have the full measure of my joy within them" (John 17:13). "Full measure"—and
Jesus doesn't exaggerate! Jesus prayed that these men would,
"have the full measure of my [his] joy within them." This is far
different, as well as infinitely of more value, than an emotional
high.

He is not saying they would escape the hard things of life, the
loss of a loved one, persecution, or the drudgery of life. Negative things won't be gone until heaven. Just yesterday Dee and

I received two phone calls that illustrate this. One was from a friend on the East coast, considerably younger than us, who discovered her husband's dead body in their backyard. That evening we talked with friends in the Midwest who had lost their grown son to natural causes, suddenly and without warning, just a few days before.

Joy is important as we make this earthly journey and we will see it is abundantly provided. For example, when Nehemiah came back to rebuild the city of Jerusalem, he and those with him had a monumental task on their hands. They also had enemies prepared to meet them. In the midst of this, Nehemiah said, "...the joy of the Lord is your strength" (Nehemiah 8:10). A few centuries later, Jesus spoke often about joy, how we could gain the joy He experienced and that He wanted us to have.

We are emotional beings. We have highs and lows and often function in-between our high and low points. Our bodies have certain rhythms and, additionally, we have happy and sad circumstances. There are people who are close to the emotional middle much of the time, though they also have a range of emotions. Others have more dramatic highs and lows and spend less time in the emotional middle.

Here is a hypothetical situation: You and your spouse are having a "picture perfect" dinner on a Hawaiian beach as the sun is setting. You have had a wonderful day together. As you enjoy the balmy breezes, you listen to the ocean gently splash against the rocks. Just before you left for dinner you heard the stock market had gone up 300 points and on your voice mail was a message from your boss telling you about a 10 percent raise in your salary. Back home, all your children know the Lord and, during a recent phone conversation with them, you learned your only grandchild had just accepted Christ. In fact no one in your immediate family struggles with physical ailments or spiritual deficiencies. How good it all feels! Enjoy it. Don't say to yourself: "I wonder when the next shoe will fall." Soak it up, thank God for moments like these, and don't read the obituaries to see how many have died who are your age or younger!

Conversely, the Bible tells us we will have hard experiences. Romans 8:17 says, "Now if we are children, then we are heirs—heirs of God and co-heirs with Christ, if indeed we share in his sufferings in order that we may also share in his glory." Philippians 1:29 says it a different way: "For it has been granted to you on behalf of Christ not only to believe on him, but also to suffer for him." Life is a mix. Learn to live with the mix and also to practice godliness with contentment which Scripture says is great gain (1 Timothy 6:6). Paul said in Philippians 4:11-13,

> ...I have learned to be content whatever the circumstances. I know what it is to be in need, and I know what it is to have plenty. I have learned the secret of being content in any and every situation, whether well fed or hungry, whether living in plenty or in want.

Is this possible? Is this a reasonable expectation? The next verse is, "I can do everything through him who gives me strength." But note, "I have learned..."—it didn't come with conversion. He had to learn it.

The saddest day in my life turned out to be a very happy day. Our family was meeting for lunch at a restaurant after church. Dee, our son, Todd, and I were there on time but not our daughter, Kristen. Todd called and woke her up. She was home napping after attending our early church service. She told Todd she would be at the restaurant in a few minutes. After enough time for her to arrive had passed, we were concerned. You know how it is—you have a hunch, you fear the worst. We quickly finished our meal and headed out, only to see her car in the middle of the road, squashed into a ball of steel. We were there just minutes after the collision but she had already been taken away. We could see her shoe on the road and a policeman sweeping up glass and other parts of the compressed, demolished car. My heart sank. How could anyone in that car have survived? Filled with fear and panic, I asked the policeman if she was alive. He said, "Yes." I didn't know if he was trying to give me hope or if he had seen her alive. He told me where they had taken her. She came into the hospital as "Jane Doe—Code Blue."

The three of us raced to the hospital. The trip was surreal. Was she alive? I had never been this frightened. I prayed out loud and fervently, "Dear Lord, please let Kristen live." Nothing was important to me at that moment except Kristen—our only daughter, born just seventeen years, one month and five days before. Like most parents, we adore our children. They mean everything to us. That's why words fail me in trying to explain how I felt. I would far rather die than have her die. If we lost her, I wanted God to take me home to heaven as well. I could not imagine life without either of our children. A feeling of happiness was nowhere to be found in my life at that moment. I was overwhelmed with sorrow. I trusted God with all my heart and knew He would do the right thing. But, what if the right thing was to take Kristen's life? I would still trust God but I would be one of the saddest people on earth.

We ran into the hospital. The waiting room was already

filled with people from the church I served as pastor. They had heard about the accident and were there waiting, praying, loving—wanting to be there when we arrived. My emotions were in the basement—feeling nothing that resembled happiness. I went through doors I was not supposed to go through to see if Kristen was alive. She was! She was surrounded by a wonderful medical team standing almost shoulder-to-shoulder. Two more surgeons were on their way to put her back together—one to start at one end of her body and another to start at the other. "Is she going to make it?" was my all-consuming question. I called my mother and dad and told them of the accident, telling them I didn't know if Kristen was going to live. They went immediately to prayer.

When I found out her prognosis was guarded but good, my joy was as high as my sadness had been low a few minutes before. What was wrong with me the day of Kristen's accident? Where was my joy? Was there something lacking in my Christian experience? The only way I could have been more heartbroken is if she had not lived. My emotions at that moment were not a good indication of "the joy of my salvation." It was a response of love. My faith was solid in God but I was heartbroken over my daughter.

Throughout Scripture, joy is a major issue and verses that reference it are widespread. Here are just a few from the Old and New Testaments: Deuteronomy 16:15; 1 Chronicles 16:27; Psalm 4:7, 21:6, 30:11, 43:4, 107:22; Proverbs 10:1, 28, 12:20; Isaiah 55:12; Luke 2:10; John 3:29; 2 Corinthians 8:2; Philippians 2:2, 4:1; 1 Thessalonians 2:19; Philemon 7; Hebrews 12:2; 1 Peter 1:8; and 2 John 4.

It is God's way that works! Many times Dee and I have said

at the end of a movie, "This was another proof that the only good way to live, the only way life works well, is the way God has laid out for us." Ungodly things may seem as though they have a lot to offer but when all is said and done, "...the way of the unfaithful is hard" (Proverbs 13:15). In stark contrast to those who think following Christ is difficult, or that the obedient life has everything pleasant drained out, we see the opposite is true. We become recipients of His joy.

The well-known statesman Malcolm Muggeridge first met Mother Teresa in Calcutta where she chose to labor for so many years among destitute and dying people. He could not explain the "luminous quality" he saw in this small, dedicated woman. Her joy was used by God to draw him to Christ. Her joy is an example of what our Lord promised 2,000 years ago. He always shares His joy with those who obey Him. "...I say these things while I am still in the world, so that they may have the full measure of my joy within them" (John 17:13).

If we want to avoid a barren and cheerless existence and have the joy that Christ offers, we get it by obeying His commands and that, by the way, will include living a fruitful life. It will be within the providence, permission, and supervision of God, including some suffering along the way.

Jesus Calls Us into Joy

In the churches I have served, I have noted the most joyful people are those who are immersed in the work of Christ in and out of the church. It must have been that way in the Old Testament as well. I have also noticed people who come to church simply to find good friends or business contacts like it is a Christian country club. They are typically unhappy and don't understand that, in addition to the church being a place for worship, it is also a command post for local, national, and global evangelism—it is a place for serious Bible study, discipleship, starting new churches, and reaching out to those in need.

Jesus told us where joy is found. He wrote the rules. He is the one who created us and decided how things work. In the midst of living as He prescribes, we may not experience a Disneyland emotional high (Can you tell I like going there?) but our joy can be full. We gain it by losing our life—putting our agendas aside—for the sake of Christ and then we find real living. "For whoever wants to save his life will lose it, but whoever loses his life for me will save it" (Luke 9:24).

A primary reason for Jesus coming to a helpless, hopeless, and sinful humanity was to offer a sweeping change for those who wanted it. "…I have come that they may have life, and have it to the full" (John 10:10). This is a big issue to Jesus. He wants joyful disciples. The negative, pessimistic Christians who look like they drank vinegar for breakfast are not living out the kind of life Christ has offered.

Are feelings involved in the Christian experience? Absolutely! But it is different than emotional highs. Those emotional highs are encouraging and often abundantly helpful but the joy Christ gives us exceeds emotional highs in unending worth and enduring fulfillment. G.K. Chesterton called our joy "the gigantic secret of the Christian."

Ask for Joy

And now, another twist to joy. Jesus is telling us to ask Him for it. Have you ever considered that? "Until now you have not asked for anything in my name. Ask and you will receive, and your joy will be complete" (John 16:24). Joy must be included in the "anything." Jesus is again talking about complete joy. Have you asked? God is very interested in meeting our needs and giving His people joy. Because we are to ask, and because prayer is talking to God, prayer is connected to our joy. Unlike parents, who are sometimes annoyed by the incessant questions of small children, God has a fondness for our coming to Him frequently in prayer. The verse begins, "Until now you have not asked for anything in my name." It is His name on the check that opens up untold wealth. This abundance has many facets and one of them is joy.

Harry Ironside, the much loved pastor and Bible expositor of several decades ago, told the story of a young man dying on the battlefield of the Civil War:

Another soldier nearby crawled to him and found this poor boy in dreadful condition and did everything he could to help him. They talked together, and then the soldier said, "Now, if I get out alive, is there anything I could do for you?" "Well," the injured man said, "maybe I can do something for you. My father is wealthy, and if you get through this conflict alive, and are ever in need, take this little card (and he wrote a few words on it) and go to see my father, and I know he will be ready to help you out." The soldier did not think he would ever use the card, but the time came when he was in dire need, and he remembered the conversation. He did as this dying man suggested and found his father, a wealthy man. Through the underlings and secretaries, he sent in his own card and got no response. And then he thought of the other card and got it out, and on it was written these words, "Father, if you can ever do anything for my friend who helped me when I was dying, please do so." It was signed "Charlie." In a moment, out came the big business man and he said, "Oh, why didn't you send that in before? I will do anything that I can for you for Charlie's sake!" (H.A. Ironside, *John*. Loizeaux Brothers Inc., 1942)

God loves to have us ask and do things for us for Jesus' sake. He is our heavenly Father!

 I heard a speaker who illustrated prayer by telling us that when he was a boy his grandfather told him anytime he wanted a nickel, he could come to him and get one. He often went for his nickel. He wondered why his grandfather didn't give him more money so he wouldn't have to keep bothering him for nickels. As the boy grew older, he realized his grandfather enjoyed spending time with him so he liked to have him keep coming for another nickel. Jesus went so far as to say, "pray continually" (1 Thessalonians 5:17).

Why don't we ask? Have we overlooked 1 John 5:14-15? "This is the confidence we have in approaching God: that if we ask anything according to his will, he hears us. And if we know that he hears us—whatever we ask—we know that we have what we asked of him." Or, the often-quoted James 4:2: "...You do not have, because you do not ask God."

Joy That Stays Despite Our Circumstances

We must be careful not to confuse joy with an emotional high. Emotional highs come and go. The deep-seated joy Jesus promised comes and stays as we live the life He modeled for us. It is interesting Jesus spoke more about joy the closer He came to the cross. For Jesus, hanging on the cross was a major reason for His coming to earth, though it was not an emotional high. The Garden of Gethsemane was not an emotional high: "And being in anguish, he prayed more earnestly, and his sweat was like drops of blood falling to the ground" (Luke 22:44). It was not an emotional high when He said: "My soul is overwhelmed with sorrow to the point of death," nor when He fell to the ground and earnestly prayed that, if possible, the hour might pass from Him (Mark 14:34-35).

Joy is an immense word—it is so many things! It is pondering what God has done for us. It is enjoying His provisions every day and resting in the belief that He will continue to provide. Joy is knowing we are doing the will of God. It is seeing someone come into the salvation experience. In the midst of this, we have some terrible experiences living in a broken, sinful world, but our joy is in our hope of Christ's return; our confidence of His taking care of us and sending angels to serve us, to know all our sins are forgiven, that we are God's children, that He makes everything turn out for good. The list goes on and on and on. First Peter 4:12-14 adds:

> Dear friends, do not be surprised at the painful trial you are suffering, as though something strange were happening to you. But rejoice that you participate in the suf-

ferings of Christ, so that you may be overjoyed when his
glory is revealed. If you are insulted because of the name
of Christ, you are blessed, for the Spirit of glory and of
God rests on you.

I have made a list of things I am thankful for. This is a list
I can look at when I'm not feeling thankful and need an emotional lift. Ruminating on your list and thanking God for each
item unhurriedly is great tonic! What we are really doing when
we do this is thinking of and thanking God for who He is and
what He does for us.

During my first pastorate, at age 29, I traveled to Ethiopia.
Perhaps my biggest surprise was observing that the people there
seemed happier than most Americans. Not many years ago, I
was in the Cameroons of Africa where I met a dear woman who
said, "I thank God that He has given me all I need." I later found
out she lived in a mud hut and had only a small plot of land for
a garden where she grew her food. Of course, she had no auto-
mobile, no air conditioning—not even a bicycle or the hope of
owning one. She had no central heating, just a fire in the middle
of her hut with a hole in the roof for the smoke to escape. Yet,
she was praising God for His abundant provisions. How different from the flippant sign I saw in a tourist shop: "I have been
rich and I have been poor. Rich is better." Worse than that is the
bumper sticker that says, "The person who dies with the most
toys wins."

I take for granted I have central heating and air conditioning on an automatic thermostat that ensures, before I even get
up, the temperature is perfect. A couple decades ago, I made
my first trip to India. The poverty deeply gripped my soul. I

wrestled with how the Lord would want me to deal with the disparity between my life and the lives I witnessed in India. My conscience was pricked; I could not reconcile this disparity.

Similarly, I remember two brothers from my youth who were called "misers" by the people in my community. I hadn't known any people called misers until I worked with one of the brothers on a farm. He would save his toothpick after the meal. I have a clear recollection of him sticking it in his overalls when he finished using it. When he received a paycheck, he walked five miles into town to deposit it, even though he and his brother owned an old car and gasoline was about 27 cents a gallon! At home they turned the kerosene lamp very low while they strained to read the newspaper in order to conserve kerosene. Electricity was an unnecessary luxury. They were well-to-do financially— they just lived as though they were poor.

I fear many live as spiritual paupers when they could live spiritually affluent. People sometimes live as spiritual refugees and beggars rather than enjoying our divine wealth in Christ. Let's see how this works. The psalmist wrote in Psalm 68:3: "But may the righteous be glad and rejoice before God; may they be happy and joyful." James writes: "Is any one of you in trouble? He should pray. Is anyone happy? Let him sing songs of praise" (James 5:13).

Something that has been of great joy to me is quoting to myself or Dee when we get up in the morning, "This is the day the Lord has made; let us rejoice and be glad in it" (Psalm 118:24). This is obviously our own choice to make each day.

Summary of Chapter 8

Are Feelings Part of Assurance?

I was still in elementary school when I heard testimonies like: "I came to Christ 40 years ago and I have been happy ever since." Perhaps they were telling the truth but they must have had a different view of "happy" than I had. It caused me to doubt my salvation. I had come to the Lord as a child with childlike faith but I wasn't happy all the time. There are feelings associated with salvation. They are part of our assurance; but they are far different than a child's view of "happy."

Romans 8:16, "The Spirit himself testifies with our spirit that we are God's children," is a verse that troubled me. What does the Spirit testifying with my spirit feel like? How much of it did I need to have? How do I know if what I feel is what I'm supposed to feel? Properly understood, Romans 8:16 can be one of the most helpful verses on assurance in the New Testament. It has been for me. *expand*

It is important to mention we have all been created differently with a wide range in emotional capacities. Some people are very emotional and expressive while others are more stoic with a modest emotional range. Our God-given personalities influence how we experience and express spiritual realities.

For Christians, in addition to the Romans 8:16 insight, there are many reasons for joy. John 15, 16, and 17 talk about joy and the reasons for it. We have life experiences that lift us up and others that take us down. God works in and through them all. We shouldn't be surprised that our emotions are impacted.

The key to living the most joyful life, with the most

contentment and satisfaction, is to not only trust in Christ as Savior and Lord but also to live the way the Scriptures outline. God made us and He wrote the rules for the best way to live— the really good life. He has even told us: "...Ask and you will receive, and your joy will be complete" (John 16:24). Earlier in that verse Jesus said: "Until now you have not asked for any- thing in my name..." It seems that "joy" must be included in the "anything" we ask for. Jesus understands our joys and sorrows. He experienced both while He was in His incarnate state in this world.

Personal Reflection or Discussion Questions

1. What is the difference between joy and happiness?

2. How can feelings get in the way of our assurance of salvation?

3. How can feelings help us in the assurance of salvation? Give two ways mentioned in this chapter.

4. Are you ever sad? Is this an indication of not having salvation?

5. What is a cure for sadness?

Chapter 9

What If a Person Has Not Been Predestined for Salvation?

John 6:37

During the critical moments following the assassination attempt on his life, President Reagan did not lose his sense of humor. He told those tending to him, "I hope you guys are all Republicans!" He received a kind response: "Today, we're all Republicans." He said to his wife, Nancy, "Honey, I forgot to duck!" *(Title)– That's where I got the title for sermon*

As we read Scripture and come to words like "predestined," "chosen," and "elected," it is important we don't "duck" or try to make them say something other than their clear meaning. We must avoid overstating, understating, or the tendency to use only those verses that support our position. If God had intended to use other words, He would have. It is by inspiration of God the Holy Spirit that the words in Scripture are there.

The subject of predestination, God predetermining things of the future, has troubled many, including me, and remains a contentious topic. Sometimes I wonder if those overly passionate on the subject are motivated by scholarship, a sincere effort to resolve the issue, fear in their own life, or the love of a good argument. Whatever the reason, let's look at it with our best objectivity. My primary concerns are an accurate interpretation of Scripture and helping Christians and seekers understand the often confusing doctrine of predestination. I'll explore a biblical answer to this question, along with other legitimate questions regarding predestination and our personal relationship with Christ. After looking at Scripture, we'll discover the doctrine of predestination gives us further assurance of our salvation, rather than it being a hindrance to our faith.

None of us can know the whole mind of an infinite God. Let God's Word be the final authority on what is true, not our logic. " 'For my thoughts are not your thoughts, neither are your ways my ways,' declares the Lord. 'As the heavens are higher than the earth, so are my ways higher than your ways and my thoughts than your thoughts' " (Isaiah 55:8-9). If we allow Scripture to speak for itself, a lot of problems will be taken care of when it comes to interpreting specific verses.

Let me add a very important and rather parenthetical statement. Has it struck you what a privilege we have in possessing the written Word of God? In this Word, God revealed Himself. In this Word, He gave us the redemptive plan of God in Christ Jesus. Think of the many human-made religions of the world that have huge followings, whose gods are unrevealed because they are not real. For God to disclose Himself through His Word is an incredible gift to us. The size of this gift should propel us to spend time regularly reading and meditating upon the Bible.

Let the Scripture Speak

In terms of predestination and our salvation, it is important that we not force an explanation. Let the Scripture speak. Here is where we are particularly fortunate. While we are not able to completely understand predestination, we will see that Scripture lets us know if we are personally predestined. The Appendix contains additional information on the two differing historical doctrinal movements: Calvinism and Arminianism. Rereading Chapter 3 will be helpful to be assured you are among those who have met God's requirements for salvation. It doesn't take much thought to realize this is the single most important thing in life to know. I have spent a lot of time wrestling with how people can go from "I don't know," "I think so," "I hope so," or even, "I'm 99 percent sure," to helping them know with 100 percent certainty they are going to heaven.

If we have doubts about our salvation, we should not be ashamed of them. They are the other side of belief. If one has no belief, he or she will have no doubts. I had one doubt after another. I was genuinely scared about not being predestined. As shared already, I would have said I was 90 percent sure, maybe 99 percent. Even if there was a one percent chance of my not going to heaven, I couldn't live with that. I had accepted the Lord, over and over, just to be sure. I had rededicated my life to Him repeatedly—and still do. I was like Peter answering the

Lord, "Lord, to whom shall we go? You have the words of eternal life" (John 6:68).

When Satan comes with doubts, whether today or just before we are translated into heaven, we will have an answer to give him from Scripture, as Jesus did when He was being tempted in the wilderness. In Matthew 4 it says Jesus answered the devil's temptations with Scripture, "It is written... [Verse 4], It is also written... [Verse 7], It is written... [Verse 10]."

In dealing with predestination, I will use what is written in Scripture rather than human logic. Western logic, based on Aristotelian or Socratic logic, does not rule Scripture! God is not subservient to our logic. I don't understand the "logic" of people saying of a scriptural doctrine, "That isn't logical." They aren't God! Is it any surprise that we do not know as much as God? So, the Bible rules!

Webster's Encyclopedic Unabridged Dictionary of the English Language says in their theological definition of predestination: "The action of God in foreordaining from eternity whatever comes to pass." Being fair with Scripture, we must recognize the Bible speaks frequently of predestination including people being predestined. Whether or not this fits our system of theology or our system of logic, my plea is to take Scripture at its word. If we don't, whose word do we take? Ours? Another person's? The point is, the Bible clearly speaks of predestination and we must do the same.

Predestination Is a Hidden Blessing

For our time of living or dying, predestination provides rich blessing in the assurance of our salvation. I had never thought of it that way until one day in seminary. As I was walking with my roommate, he said, "I get joy from the doctrine of predestination because if it wasn't for predestination, none of us would be saved." That thought gave me joy, too, because we are all sinners by birth and practice (read carefully Romans 3:10ff). There is nothing good in us that would cause us to come in faith and repentance to Christ. We come because He predestined us.

He chose us.
"For he chose us in him before the creation of the world" (Ephesians 1:4).

"Therefore, as God's chosen people..." (Colossians 3:12).

"...from the beginning God chose you to be saved" (2 Thessalonians 2:13).

God elected us.
"And he will send his angels with a loud trumpet call, and they will gather his elect from the four winds, from one end of the heavens to the other" (Matthew 24:31).

He predestined us.
"he predestined us to be adopted as his sons through Jesus Christ" (Ephesians 1:5).

Rather than being frustrated by these verses, believe them. In fact, enjoy them. Allowing Scripture to speak for itself, without making it fit into a theological system (such as Calvinism or Arminianism), will give you comfort. These verses tell us the only reason we came to Christ is because He chose us—He predestined us for salvation. Again, had He not chosen us, with nothing good in us, we would not have chosen Him.

Free Will and Human Responsibility

Some will counter this clear biblical teaching by saying: "This goes against our free will." The phrase "free will" is used in the Old Testament regarding some of the sacrificial rites but is not used in the Bible related to our salvation. Despite the popularity of the phrase and its influence on our theology, "free will" is absent. The issue of predestination and free will has been vigorously discussed and debated for centuries.

Dr. Bob Smith explained our inability to bring predestination and our will together by comparing each of them to a railroad track, with the tracks running parallel. Mile after mile they never come together. Smith explained that predestination and our will are both true but the two doctrines will never come together in our minds. However, they come together in the mind of God. Is there tension in our minds between predestination and our will? Yes. As one of my seminary professors said, "Let the tension remain." We don't need to resolve it. God's ways and thoughts are higher than ours (Isaiah 55:8-9). Let the Scripture speak for itself.

While there is predestination, there is also human

responsibility. There are numerous verses that clearly state we have to make a decision. For example, in John 1:12 it says: "Yet to all who received him, to those who believed in his name, he gave the right to become children of God."

Another responsibility is to tell the Gospel to the whole world. This is our duty. Note Romans 10:14 and Christ's final recorded words in Acts 1:8. Just as John, in John 1:29, introduced Jesus by saying, "...Look, the Lamb of God, *who takes away the sin of the world*" (emphasis mine), we, too, need to make Him known. There are many commands to witness and to be involved in global evangelism. That is another tension that must be considered alongside the biblical teaching of predestination.

Why have such aggressive programs of evangelism if people are elected and are going to be saved by the drawing of the Holy Spirit? The answer is obedience. He told us to in Matthew 28:19-20. "Therefore go and make disciples of all nations, baptizing them in the name of the Father and of the Son and of the Holy Spirit, and teaching them to obey everything I have commanded you. And surely I am with you always, to the very end of the age." A heartwarming and challenging factor in being involved in global evangelism is that we are joining Christ in the only recorded prayer request given Him by His Heavenly Father. "Ask of me, and I will make the nations your inheritance, the ends of the earth your possession" (Psalm 2:8).

Being predestined does not excuse us from other responsibilities. For example, in 2 Peter 1:5-7 we are told to: "...*make every effort* to add to your faith goodness; and to goodness, knowledge; and to knowledge, self-control; and to self-control, perseverance; and to perseverance, godliness; and to godliness, brotherly kindness; and to brotherly kindness, love," (emphasis mine). We

7. cannot hide behind our view of predestination because the next move, according to His Word, is ours.

Complete Belief, Though Not Complete Understanding

Those with allegiance to a particular theological system, or to a view that has to be consistent with their logic, sometimes find it difficult to hold to a clear and simple biblical view. Remember, certain people were inspired by the Holy Spirit to write the Bible for each of us to read. Further, because it is God's Word for all people, we can be assured He has supervised the process of the Scriptures coming to us through many generations and civilizations. It is vital that we take the Scripture for what it says and let any tension—places we don't understand and can't reconcile—remain. We do not understand it all but we can believe it all.

For example, predestination is true because Scripture uses that word. A primary use of this word in the Scriptures is God predestinating His people for salvation. Regardless of how we might prefer God to work with His people, we should let the Scripture speak for itself and believe it. Of course, that means we take all of Scripture—the Bible is its own best interpreter. It is a life-long task to understand the Scriptures. Even at the end of life, we will not understand with the perfection we long to have—that will take place in heaven.

We need to allow the Bible to give us its clear meaning. Most verses are easy to understand. However, there are places and theological areas that require our best study skills. A point to remember is to take the obvious meaning when it is there, and it usually can be found. When we come to difficult places, such as predestination, we look at other verses that use the same word, as well as synonyms, and place them beside verses that seem to say something else. To the best of our ability, and in reliance on the Holy Spirit for illumination, we try to discover what God wants us to know.

Verses on Predestination

For now, let's look at more verses on predestination and allow them to speak to us.

"For he chose us in him before the creation of the world to be holy and blameless in his sight. In love he predestined us to be adopted as his sons through Jesus Christ, in accordance with his pleasure and will" (Ephesians 1:4-5).

"In him we were also chosen, having been predestined according to the plan of him who works out everything in conformity with the purpose of his will" (Ephesians 1:11).

There is a parallel word "chose," or "chosen" (the latter also in Ephesians 1:11). Note also the following:

"But we ought always to thank God for you, brothers loved by the Lord, because from the beginning God chose you to be saved through the sanctifying work of the Spirit and through belief in the truth" (2 Thessalonians 2:13).

"No one can come to me unless the Father who sent me draws him" (John 6:44).

I find it impossible to read the ninth chapter of Romans without seeing the predestinating hand of God. Also take a look at Romans 8:29-30:

"For those God foreknew he also predestined to be conformed to the likeness of his Son, that he might be the firstborn among many brothers. And those he predestined, he also called; those he called, he also justified; those he justified, he also glorified."

Then note these additional verses:

"You did not choose me, but I chose you." (John 15:16)

"...you do not belong to the world, but I have chosen you out of the world" (John 15:19).

"All that the Father gives me will come to me" (John 6:37).

"...This is why I told you that no one can come to me unless the Father has enabled him" (John 6:65).

"When the Gentiles heard this, they were glad and honored the word of the Lord; and all who were appointed for eternal life believed" (Acts 13:48).

Our authority is Scripture.

You Can Have Assurance of Salvation

Whatever your view on predestination, you can know you are going to heaven. How? Scripture gives clear statements that allow us to know we are going to heaven even though by nature and choice we are sinners. "It does not, therefore, depend on man's desire or effort, but on God's mercy" (Romans 9:16). Also read Romans 3:10-18, 23. First Corinthians 2:14 says:

> The man without the Spirit does not accept the things that come from the Spirit of God, for they are foolishness to him, and he cannot understand them, because they are spiritually discerned.

In our natural sinful state, we are helpless. None seek God and none are good. The only reason any of us ever desires to come to Christ is because we are drawn by the Holy Spirit. "No one can come to me unless the Father who sent me draws him, and I will raise him up at the last day" (John 6:44). This fact alone should give us assurance of salvation. If you and I want to place our faith in Christ, it is because we are elected—predestined! The Bible tells us if we want to come to Christ, it is because He is drawing us. If He is drawing us, we can come.

Verses that also support this include: John 3:16, Romans

Predestination based on foreknowledge of God [handwritten]

10:13, Revelation 22:17 and a host of others. John 6:37 in a very interesting way speaks of both predestination and the fact that anyone who wants to come can come. It is a strong statement that while predestination is involved, it does not limit anyone who wants to come to Christ. "All that the Father gives me will come to me, and whoever comes to me I will never drive away." How can this be anything other than those called of God will come and will be received by God when they choose to come?

There are scores of verses that say anyone who calls, or whoever wills, can be saved. Rather than making these verses fit into the Arminian column or the Calvinist column, it is better to let them be an assurance to us that we are, indeed, part of God's redeemed family. Regardless of your view, you can look at these verses and say, "I called," or, "I believe," so obviously I am part of God's redeemed family. For example, read the following:

> "For God so loved the world that he gave his one and only Son, that whoever believes in him shall not perish but have eternal life." John 3:16

> "And everyone who calls on the name of the Lord will be saved." Acts 2:21

> "The Spirit and the bride say, 'Come!' And let him who hears say, 'Come!' Whoever is thirsty, let him come; and whoever wishes, let him take the free gift of the water of life." Revelation 22:17

Regardless of our theological position on predestination, the issue of our own salvation is settled if we are willing to come to Christ. It has to be this way to be consistent with the great number of verses in Scripture that leave the door wide open for whoever wants to come to Christ. They can come! Is the Bible true? Then "everyone who calls on the name of the Lord will be saved" (Romans 10:13). In verse 17 of the final book and chapter of the Bible, it again says the door is wide open to anyone who wants to come to Christ. This is a gracious verse that has been of particular blessing to me. There is no limitation or restrictions to those who want to come to Christ.

Take What You Do Understand

We can't understand all there is to know about God drawing us to salvation. We can't know why some, and not others, are drawn to Christ by the Holy Spirit in such a way that they place their trust in Him. We should take what we do understand and leave the rest to a merciful, just, and loving God. When we get to heaven we will fully understand, but not until then.

Something else I cannot figure out is why do some seemingly dedicated Christians leave the Christian community and live an ungodly life until their death? Living like Christ wants His children to live is the best, most peaceful and happy life in the world. Why would anyone trade down? It's like trading your new BMW for a 1948 Studebaker! The only light on this that I have found is 1 John 2:19 which we have already considered.

Can anyone who wants to come to Christ come? Yes!—a thousand times yes! Regardless of sins committed and regardless of believing in or not believing in predestination.

Summary of Chapter 9

What If a Person Has Not Been Predestined for Salvation?

Hearing this question can raise a range of emotions including fear, a sense of unfairness, and internal conflict as you think about a loving God who is, "...not wanting any to perish, but everyone to come to repentance" (2 Peter 3:9).

Raising the question of predestination in public can draw a crowd of theologians who will vigorously debate each other, each with a list of Bible verses supporting their position. Let's be sure we are clear and fair. That requires us to state the Scripture's use of the word "predestination" and "chosen," along with other words that end up, given the context, to mean the same thing. Then, we must declare the Scriptures are clear in stating anyone who wants to, can become a Christian. We can't allow our logic to take precedence over the Scriptures. We must remember the verse in Isaiah 55 that tells us God's ways are higher than ours and so are His thoughts. Deuteronomy 29:29 tells us there are secret things that belong to the Lord. God is not bound to our logic. He doesn't check with humanity's various systems of thinking before He makes a decision or lays out a plan.

The doctrine of predestination unnecessarily troubled me. My dismay was simply that if God predestines people for salvation, what if I'm not predestined? I rolled this one around different ways and ultimately came to a similar conclusion that I came to with the unpardonable sin. While I do not understand everything about predestination, I do know that I am predestined. Why? Because of the numerous verses that tell us that anyone who wants to come to Christ can come and I wanted to come. There are no qualifiers to those verses such as, "provided you have been predestined." A very difficult theological issue becomes very simple as it relates to someone who wants to be saved. Right up to the end of the Scriptures, Revelation 22:17, the invitation is simple, straight forward, and available to everyone.

Predestination can be boiled down to a single sentence: "Predestination is a biblical teaching that is not possible to completely understand in this lifetime; but it in no way limits the salvation of anyone wanting to come to Christ."

I like That [1]

Why the Great Commission if He only takes the elect. —

Personal Reflection or Discussion Questions

1. How do you know you are predestined for salvation?

2. There is more information available in the Appendix, but is there anything that's become clearer to you regarding pre-destination and our own will than before?

3. Can you think of any reason why a person who wants to become a Christian cannot become one?

4. What role does logic have in our understanding of Scripture?

5. What do you do with this quote: "I know I am free, yet I see in my life a plan that is not my own"? Is this true of you?

6. How do you respond to Norman Geisler's quote: "God knows with certainty what we will freely choose"?

7. What about this (approximate) quote: "He who will can and he who can will."

8. How do you reconcile that the grossly heinous act of the crucifixion of Christ had its exact place in the plan of God? (Note Acts 2:23, 4:28)

9. Going back to Chapter 3, what is the litmus test of whether or not a person is going to heaven?

Chapter 10

You Can Trust Jesus

I am concluding this book in the midst of the greatest economic crisis in my lifetime. Twelve million people are unem-
ployed. Home foreclosures are increasing everyday. Much of this
has happened because of wealthy people who have scammed
hard-working Americans. While enriching themselves, they
caused much sorrow to others and created a feeling of helpless-
ness in America. A few days ago I read of a 90-year-old man
who lost his life savings through the largest Ponzi scheme in
American history. He had to go back to work because he does
not have enough money on which to live. There is great sorrow
and mistrust as more people are homeless and on food stamps.
This economic crisis circles the globe with no easy solutions in
sight.

In addition to the difficulties all around us, we have wrestled with some difficult biblical issues in this book. I congratulate you for getting to the last chapter. I hope and I pray that you have found spiritual answers and been able to resolve areas of doubt. If this book helps you avoid some of the struggle I went through, I will be delighted. I will also feel there was a positive purpose for going through those doubts and fears.

Let's turn a corner in overcoming doubts. Praying you have resolved your doubts, let's think about the contrast to the troubles all around us by sitting back and enjoying trusting Jesus. In the midst of chaos, I want to list a few characteristics of our Savior that are of enormous blessing to me, believing they will be to you as well.

Jesus Is Kind

What a big word "kind" is! There is no one as kind as Jesus. We are drawn to kind people. In a marriage, when husband and wife are kind to each other, their marriage will be a good one. I often talk about kindness when conducting a wedding ceremony and later, just before the bride and groom leave, I frequently go to them and say in a friendly, easy way, "Hey you two, be kind to each other." I can tell from the way they look at me, they don't understand why I give them this bit of friendly advice. However, most understand before they even get back from their honeymoon!

Jesus loved children. Can't you see Him as He picks a child up in His arms? When the blind man pleaded for Jesus to come over to him and heal him, Jesus did. When people were hungry, He

3/19/20
10:50 P. M.

fed them. He talked to people who were despised and went into
the home of sinners. He had no caste system. He chose common
people like us to be His disciples. Who else would demonstrate
His strength through our weakness (2 Corinthians 12:10)? He
did that with Peter, a man He chose as a disciple. Peter denied
Him, swore he never knew Him, and yet Jesus chose him to
preach that great message on the Day of Pentecost. Following
His resurrection, Jesus made sure that the message that He was
alive reached Peter. An angel told the women visiting the now
empty tomb, "...go, tell his disciples and Peter" (Mark 16:7). He
didn't want Peter left out. I can't help but think Peter, having
cursed and denied that he even knew who Jesus was, wondered
what his status was with his Savior. Jesus is kind. He had the
angel be sure Peter received the news of His resurrection. This
is a touching phrase in light of what had happened just days
before. It touches my soul that Jesus is my Savior, too.

The word "kindness" is included in the fruit of the Spirit
(Galatians 5:22-23). The more we demonstrate the fruit of the
Spirit, the more we are like Jesus. Jesus is kind to us and invites
us to respond to His offer:

> Come to me, all you who are weary and burdened, and
> I will give you rest. Take my yoke upon you and learn
> from me, for I am gentle and humble in heart, and you
> will find rest for your souls. For my yoke is easy [or, my
> yoke fits!] and my burden is light (Matthew 11:28-30).

Just this morning in my devotions I was reading about the
infinite love that God has for you and me. It is an incredible
thing—think about it! "For as high as the heavens are above the

earth [How high is that?], so great is his love for those who fear him; as far as the east is from the west [How far is that?], so far has he removed our transgressions from us" (Psalm 103:11-12). Our attempts to describe His kindness fail us; our adjectives are inadequate. It seems easier to believe Jesus is infinitely kind to others more than to us. Ponder His kindness to you…not just to others.

Jesus Is Gracious

Jesus didn't have to die for our sins—it was His choice. Think about His struggle for us as He prayed in Gethsemane. Luke, the physician, described it this way: "And being in anguish, he prayed more earnestly, and his sweat was like drops of blood falling to the ground" (Luke 22:44). What must it have been like for a physician to use that kind of language?

Christ made His decision. It was consistent with why He came to earth. Crucifixion was terrible, reserved for the worst of criminals. Add to that the scoffing and scorn, the crown of thorns, and His mother standing by watching along with John, his very close friend. There, with the eastern, scorching sun likely beating down on Him, He was on display for all to see and ridicule. He did it for us. Why? He is gracious, infinitely gracious. When He cried out: "It is finished" (John 19:30), He was saying the payment for our redemption was complete. He died the death we should have died, but only He could do it. As the Irish hymn writer, C.F. Alexander, wrote: "There was no other good enough to pay the price of sin. He only could unlock the door of heaven and let us in." Jesus, the one without sin, had the sins of the world laid on Him, "...the Lord has laid on him the iniquity of us all" (Isaiah 53:6). This may have been the most painful part of the crucifixion—and perhaps the reason His Father turned His face from Him. "About the ninth hour Jesus cried out in a loud voice, *'Eloi, Eloi, lama sabachthani?'*— which means, 'My God, my God, why have you forsaken me?' " (Matthew 27:46). He prayed for the Father to even forgive those crucifying Him. He made sure His mother was taken care of by John and then He died. Jesus is gracious.

We are the recipients of that grace that knows no bounds. "O the love that drew salvation's plan! O the grace that brought it down to man! O the mighty gulf that God did span at Calvary" (hymn: "At Calvary" by William Newell and Daniel Towner). Does that take you to your knees in gratitude? Is there anything in all of your life or in the entire world that comes close? Jesus is gracious beyond all measure and beyond all description. Think of the worst things you have done during your lifetime. Jesus has taken care of those things. He loves you and lavishes His grace upon you as much as if you had never done those things. There is nothing you could do to make Him love you more or be more gracious to you. There is no one like Jesus.

The opposite of this is selfishness—the quality common to all sin. And yet for Jesus: "My food...is to do the will of him who sent me and to finish his work" (John 4:34). Jesus chose graciousness over selfishness. Think of what He left to come to earth. Think of what was waiting for Him here. The Jewel of Heaven was rejected by those to whom He came.

Dr. Donald Barnhouse tells of when he was a little boy raised in the Midwest, the wheat field in front of his house caught on fire. The blaze began to roar, the heat was intense. He remembers shaking in the corner as he watched the fire. He stuffed his hands in his pockets that evening and walked outside, feeling the heat as it radiated from that charred field. He walked along the road kicking pieces of debris. Seeing a large chunk that looked like a piece of bark, he bumped it and little chickens ran everywhere. He leaned over and flipped what he thought was debris, and it was the charred remains of the hen that had pulled her little chicks under her wings. She died that they could live. Barnhouse pointed out, the Lord God in Christ pulled us under His wings and died so we could live. Out of mercy and in answer to the unfathomable plan of God, He provided a majestic purpose—the death of His Son that we might live.

Jesus Is Powerful and Gentle

Powerful and gentle only appear to be opposites. Jesus is the epitome of the statement: "There is no gentleness like real strength and no strength like real gentleness."

Let's muse together a bit. Jesus was present at creation, "…without him nothing was made that has been made" (John 1:3). He has always been. Before Abraham was, He was (John 8:58). Always been! My mind breaks down at that point. Jesus was not only there from eternity past and powerful enough to create the universe, but He holds it together. Scientists wonder what holds everything together. They have expressions like "nuclear glue." It's Jesus! Read Colossians 1:17.

As powerful as He is, He was also gentle when the grieving father of Matthew 9:18 came up to Him, and when the suffering woman was healed by touching the hem of His garment

(Matthew 9:20), and when He wept after His friend, Lazarus, died (John 11:35), and when He stooped so low as to take away my sins that had been laid on Him (Isaiah 53:6) and gave me eternal life. His gentleness also knows no boundaries.

There's a wideness in God's mercy,
Like the wideness of the sea;
There's a kindness in His justice,
Which is more than liberty.

There is welcome for the sinner,
And more graces for the good;
There is mercy with the Savior;
There is healing in His blood.

For the love of God is broader
Than the measure of our mind;
And the heart of the Eternal
Is most wonderfully kind.

If our love were but more simple,
We should take Him at His word;
And our lives would be all sunshine
In the sweetness of our Lord.
(Hymn: "There's a Wideness in God's Mercy" by
Frederick W. Faber)

He is powerful and He is gentle … this Savior of mine.

Trust Him More

Henrietta Mears was one of the matriarchs of the World War II generation. She founded Forest Home Conference Center, Gospel Light Publications, and personally discipled many effective servants of the Lord, including Bill Bright and Chaplain Halverson of the United States Senate. In her old age, someone asked her if she would do anything different if she had her life to live over. She said, "Yes, I would believe God."

Didn't she believe God? Wasn't her trust in Him for salvation? Yes, without question. She was saying she would trust Him even more. She had come to understand that there is no limit to the extent of how much we should trust Him.

In this day of scams and schemes, ongoing terrorist threats, and uncertainty on many fronts, is it not wonderful to trust Jesus, and then to trust Him more?

He has promised that it is His job to take care of us (Matthew 6:33). Do we believe that or do we worry? His wealth is without measure, as is His love. Do we trust or worry?

What about the stock market...our retirement accounts? What about our health? It can get worse as we worry! What about your future? He has already walked our tomorrows. He knows everything about everything. When Abraham Lincoln was a circuit riding lawyer, he stopped at an inn for the night. There had been a lot of precipitation that year and rivers were swollen. He spoke with a Methodist Presiding Bishop who was also traveling a great deal by horseback. Lincoln asked him, "If these other rivers are so swollen, what about the Fox River?" The Bishop replied, "I have one rule about the Fox River. It is that I never cross it until I get there." I heard my dad say, "I know worry helps because almost everything I've worried about has never happened." Jesus said "...do not worry about tomorrow" (Matthew 6:34). What isn't clear and wonderful about that?

Trust God's Leadership in Your Life

The psalmist said, "The Lord is my shepherd." No one can have a better one. The shepherd leads his sheep into green pastures and quiet waters (sheep are afraid of rushing waters). He is there to guide, protect, and provide even in the midst of enemies. The psalmist said because the Lord is his shepherd, he would not be in want. The shepherd provided an overflowing cup. The psalmist knew he would have goodness and love to follow him all the days of his life and he would dwell in the house of the Lord forever (Psalm 23). Sometimes when I come to that psalm in my devotions I get "stuck." Thinking and praying through all those promises and blessings in one sitting is a lot. We are, indeed, a privileged people.

God wants to lead us more than we want to be led. Why? Because He wants to arrange things for our good more than we want to turn over the controls. It is easy to pray as though we trust Him and believe in Him for everything, and still go our own way. His way is best, however, and we can look back and see how His way worked far better than our way. "It is God who arms me with strength and makes my way perfect" (Psalm 18:32). It's hard to beat a way that is perfect.

Or, how about those who live their lives looking back at their failings? In *The Person Reborn*, Paul Tournier tells of a visit from a dear friend who was having great inner turmoil. He had made a life-changing decision based on his understanding of God's will. Subsequent events, however, gave him second thoughts about his decision. Each morning Dr. Tournier and his friend read the Bible and prayed together. One day they came to Genesis 19 and the story of Lot's wife being turned into a pillar of salt because she looked back. Suddenly the distressed man said with a burst of insight, "I am like Lot's wife! My life is petrified because I keep looking back. I turn that problem over and over uselessly, without ever discovering whether I did right or not."

We can trust God to lead us into the future. Even when we aren't sure which way to go and must make a decision, we can be sure God will lead if we are committed to doing His will, whatever it is. God tells us, "I will instruct you and teach you in the way you should go; I will counsel you and watch over you" (Psalm 32:8). God leads, supervises, superintends, and guides our steps because, when our steps are correct, we get to the right place in the right way.

When Dee and I went to Chicago to meet with the Board of Trustees of the Baptist General Conference regarding the possibility of becoming the president and CEO of this wonderful denomination, we weren't sure whether we should go this direction or not. We prayed, discussed, but didn't have a clear answer. The Lord knew we were willing to take this position or not…either way, as long as it was His will. We had dialogue with the Board and then they excused us while they made a decision. They called us back and announced that they would like me to be the president, subject to the vote of the delegates. I felt I should give them an answer at that time. They had come from all over the nation and there had been much discussion with the search committee as well as other leadership. I stood up and said, "I accept."

I have long believed that knowing the will of God is more dependent upon our willingness to do the will of God, regardless of what it is, than any other factor. Even when it isn't clear to us, God cares enough and superintends our lives to the extent that we can trust even "holy hunches," as long as we do what we believe we should do.

Trust Him for Protection

It never ends—this parent thing of being concerned for our children. When our children came to the age where they could be out later than our bedtime, Dee and I made a deal with them. We could see the hall light under our bedroom door. When they came home, they were to turn it off so we could relax. We were always relieved when it clicked off. Of course we didn't realize until after our daughter was married that there were times she would come in, turn off the hall light, and go back out! From the time our children first rode their tricycle in the driveway, graduated to a bike and then—horror of horrors—got their driver's license, it was hard not to worry. My mother used to say, "Reasonable precaution and trust the Lord." She was right. After all, God loves our children more than we do. He has even dispatched angels to watch over them.

We are often more concerned about our spouse and our children than we are ourselves. We pray and trust God. We do not always know where specific danger is though we know it is all around us. This was apparent to me one time when I traveled to Rwanda. I checked in, alone, to what turned out to be a terrible hotel. I had to be careful where I stepped to avoid the cockroaches. It was dark. I was fatigued from long days and much travel and I didn't feel good about my surroundings. I pulled back the covers to discover the bedding had not been changed. I was on the first floor and could hear a group of men talking outside my window. I attempted to lock the windows but the locks didn't work. There was nothing to be done. I opened my suitcase to get my much-needed slippers and lying on top of my clothes was a slip of paper. I recognized Dee's handwriting. She had written Psalm 4:8: "I will lie down and sleep in peace, for you alone, O Lord, make me dwell in safety." That was true for me in Africa and it was true for Dee back home, half a world away.

While serving on the Biola University Board of Trustees, I heard Clyde Cook, president at the time, relate a childhood memory. He grew up in a missionary family in China during the Japanese occupation. He spoke of great fear that he had during frantic nighttime travels. His mother said, "Clyde, safety is not the absence of danger. It is the presence of God."

Enjoy Personal Assurance of Spending Eternity in Heaven

I like to think about the following story:

John Todd was born in Rutland, Vermont, into a family of several children. They later moved to the village of Killingsworth back in the early 1870s. There, at a very young age, John had both his mother and his father die and he was left without parents. The relatives wondered what to do with the number of children. They could parcel them out to other friends and family members. One dear and loving aunt said that she would take John. Charles Allan tells the moving account of little John at the age of 6, waiting for the arrival of the horse upon which the slave rode that the aunt had sent. As the slave reached down and picked up John and put him on the back, the little, bewildered, lonely boy rode off in the distance toward his aunt's home, hanging on. Allan picked up the conversation as the little boy, when night was falling, held on to the back of the slave and they talked about the home that he was going to. "Will she be there?" "Oh yeah, she'll be there waiting up for you." "Will I like living with her?" "My son, you have fallen into good hands." "Will she love me?" "Ah, she has a big heart." "Will I have my own room? Will she let me keep a puppy?" "She's got everything all set, son. I think she has some surprises for you, John." "Do you think she'll go to bed before we get there?" "Oh no," he said. "She'll be sure to wait up for you. You see, when we get out of these here woods, you'll see her candle shining in the window." Sure enough, out in the clearing, there was the candle in the window and there stood that dear woman, who reached down and lifted up that tired, bewildered lad, hugged him tightly, kissed him and said, "Welcome home." Inside there was a big fire burning in the hearth, supper on the stove. He ate a little and she took him by the hand into his new room and sat down beside him until he fell asleep. John Todd grew up to be a great minister of the Gospel. But it was there that he grew up. It was always a place of enchantment for him because of his aunt. It awed him that such a replacement existed. There was a place for him, someone waiting for him. He left a house of death and she had given him a second home. Years later, long after he moved away, she wrote with a quivering hand to tell him that death was near. Her faith was falling low and she wondered what was to become of her. This is what he wrote to her:

My dear Aunt,

Years ago when I was a boy, I left a house of death, not knowing where I was to go, whether anyone cared, whether it was the end of me. The ride was long and the slave had courage. Finally he pointed out your candle to me and there we were in the yard and there you stood, embracing me and taking me by the hand into my own room that you had made up. After all these years, I can't believe it. You did all that for me. I was expected; I felt safe in that room, so welcome, it was my room. Now it's your turn to go. And, as one who has tried it out, I'm writing to let you know someone is waiting now. Your room is all ready. The light is on. The door is open. As you ride into the yard, don't worry Auntie, you are expected. I know. I once saw God standing in your doorway, long ago.

You Can Trust Jesus

Some things in this book have been difficult to write about and to understand. However, the big issue is not hard to write about and it is not difficult to understand. It is, you can trust Jesus. There are so many disappointments in life. It is wonderful to know Jesus is trustworthy and not only will He never let you down, He will always do what He says He will do.

It is hard when a friend fails us. Divorce is devastating. We have heard that power corrupts and absolute power corrupts absolutely. We see these things on a regular basis. We can always trust Jesus. "Always" and "never" are words that should be carefully and seldom used. However, Jesus always does what He says He will do and Jesus never fails.

We fail. One evening I was taking care of our four grandchildren, including cooking dinner for them. It was time to eat and they were ready! I asked them what they wanted and they agreed on waffles. I was a bit relieved because, although I had never made them from scratch, I was sure it was simple. They were already heading for the table when I pulled out the large, economy size of Bisquick. The recipe on the box called for 18 cups of Bisquick. "That's quite a bit," I thought, but then I didn't work for Bisquick. "They know their product," I thought and so I got a bigger bowl and put in the 18 cups. The recipe also called for nine eggs and six cups of milk which I added. There was so much wet powder in the bowl. I finally decided to check the recipe, only to discover that I had been reading off the "Restaurant double sheet cake" recipe. My nine-year-old grandson said,

"Papa Bob, I know how to do it," and my job was over and his began. They've never asked me to cook again! Their confidence in my cooking weakened that day. But, we can trust Jesus.

A number of years ago Billy Graham Associate Evangelist Joe Blinco and I conducted a wedding together. It was near the end of Joe's life and a brain tumor had diminished his ability to do the outstanding things of previous years. The wedding was at Forest Home Conference Grounds. Mrs. Blinco was the wedding hostess. As is typical at weddings, there was a flurry of activity just before the wedding began. Mrs. Blinco had told me she didn't know how Joe would respond or what he could do, but just use him as best I could. One of the things Joe hadn't lost was a big view of God—he trusted Jesus! At one point, just before the wedding when things were moving at a fast and somewhat nervous pace, Joe said to his wife, "Sweetheart, who's the big one?" She said, "Oh, Joe honey, it's God." Joe smiled and said, "That's right."

We can trust Jesus.

Personal Reflection or Discussion Questions

1. What is there about trusting Christ that is most important to you?

2. What questions do you still have about your eternal life?

3. How can you share what Christ has done for you with others?

4. What causes you the most anxiety (e.g. your children, your health)?

5. What else is there, beyond what's listed in this chapter, that you enjoy most about knowing Christ?

6. Do you know doubts, whether yours or another person's, which have not been covered in this book? If so, explore additional resources at www.assurancebooks.com which will be continually updated. This information will be useful if there is a second printing of this book, minus any names. You can also send us doubts you would like covered in a second printing through the mail (names optional) by sending them to:

> Assurance Books
> P.O. Box 1747
> Thousand Oaks, California 91358

Conclusion

Thank you for reading this book. Because I am convinced that there are many struggling alone with doubts about their salvation, concerned about what will happen to them when they die, I challenge you to help others with the contents in this book. Talk to others about this issue and be open with your own experience as many struggle in silence. If you have opportunity, teach and preach on this subject—God can use you to change lives.

You can become actively involved in helping others by being part of our assurance website. Go to www.assurancebooks.com and share your experiences and insights. A significant percentage, perhaps even a majority of Christians are troubled by this issue of doubt. There is a wide range of wrestling…all the way from an occasional doubt to an obsessive doubting which casts a shadow over much of their life, limits their joyful service for Christ, and impedes their anticipation of His return. If you have been helped by the contents of this book, then I encourage you to help others be *Assured of Heaven*.

Calvinist or Arminian?

Calvinism and Arminianism and their positions on predestination and free will have been debated for two millenniums and it appears the debate will not end until the Lord returns. It is not my intention in one book to attempt settling the matter but my goal is to provide helpful information. Remember you can be a sincere and effective Christian regardless of whether you are a Calvinist (e.g. believing God elects to eternal salvation), an Arminian (e.g. believing you can lose your salvation), or somewhere in-between—the key issue of faith in Jesus Christ remains the same. Keep in mind the Bible, rather than being a system of theology, is God's Word to us and is our authority in all matters of faith and practice. When people ask me if I am a Calvinist or Arminian, I answer them, "Neither, I am a biblical theologian." I believe what the Scriptures say, whether or not it fits into a defined system.

My observation is that in our world today only a small percentage of people embrace a pure form of either Calvinism or Arminianism. For example, you may consider yourself to be an Arminian in some areas, while also believing in eternal security, a position consistent with Calvinism.

The Historic Tradition of Calvinism

Calvinism has been a major part of the theology of Christians down through the centuries. *Baker's Dictionary of Theology* (Editors: Bromiley, Henry, and Harrison. Baker Book House, 1966) says, "We define predestination as the theological doctrine, primarily associated with Calvinism, which holds that from eternity God has foreordained all things which come to pass, including the final salvation or reprobation of man." This same reference indicates the broad base of support for Calvinism in the "Westminster Confession of Faith," as well as many Baptist and Congregational churches. In the Middle Ages, we see Calvinist theologians like Anselm, Lombard, Aquinas and in pre-Reformation times Wycliffe and Huss. They are followed later, during the Protestant Reformation, by men such as Luther, Calvin, Zwingli, Melanchthon, and Knox. The Puritans of England who settled in America were Calvinists as were the Covenanters of Scotland and the Huguenots of France. Approaching later times, we can add names such as Whitefield, Hodge, Dabney, Cunningham, Smith, Shedd, Strong, Kuyper, and Warfield.

The "Westminster Confession of Faith," which is a respected

standard for most of the Presbyterian and Reformed churches throughout the world, says: "God from all eternity did by the most wise and holy counsel of his own will, freely and unchangeably ordain whatsoever comes to pass: yet so as thereby neither is God the author of sin; nor is violence offered to the will of the creatures, nor is the liberty or contingency of second causes taken away, but rather established."

Origins of Arminianism

According to *Baker's Dictionary of Theology*, Jacob Arminius lived from 1560 to 1609 and was trained in the strict Reformed tradition. He developed some doubts with respect to the Calvinistic tenets on the sovereign grace of God in salvation as well as related areas. It is important to our historical understanding that his followers (called Arminians or Remonstrants) carried his views further than he had in his writings. They produced a document called "Remonstrance" which consisted of five articles. These five articles can be summed up as:

1. God elects or reproves on the basis of foreseen faith or unbelief.

2. Christ died for all men and for every man, although only believers are saved.

3. Man is so utterly depraved that Divine grace is necessary for faith or for any good deed.

4. This grace may be resisted.

5. Whether all who are truly regenerate will certainly persevere in the faith is a point that needs further investigation.

These views were discussed and then condemned in the Synod of Dort that took place in 1618 and 1619. However, these views were continued and developed in the Netherlands by several men who, under their leadership of the Arminians, became characterized by increasing differences from the traditional Reformed faith. There are 24 tenets commonly held by Arminians.

The Wesleyan branch of the Methodist Movement strongly embraced a revised form of Arminianism, sometimes called "evangelical Arminianism." This shade of Arminianism touched upon themes that are slightly different from the tenets of Calvinism (see numbers 3, 7, 8, and 9 in the 24 tenets of Arminianism in this Appendix). Let's list a comparison of Calvinism and Arminianism with great help and appreciation to *Baker's Dictionary of Theology* which I have used for help in many theological areas, most of my years of ministry.

Calvinism

The following summarizes the Calvinist position using the "T U L I P" acrostic (from *Baker's Dictionary of Theology* © 1966, used by permission of Baker Academic, a division of Baker Publishing Group).

T **Total depravity** – Sin, with which we were born, has so total-
ly taken control of us we do not have the ability or desire to
respond to God's offer of salvation. Our will, as well as our
entire being, has been made incapable of seeking after God
because of our sin. "There is no one righteous, not even one;
there is no one who understands, no one who seeks God. All
have turned away, they have together become worthless; there
is no one who does good, not even one" (Romans 3:10-12).
"...the sinful mind is hostile to God. It does not submit to
God's law, nor can it do so. Those controlled by the sinful
nature cannot please God" (Romans 8:7-8). "The god of this
age has blinded the minds of unbelievers, so that they cannot
see the light of the gospel of the glory of Christ, who is the
image of God" (2 Corinthians 4:4).

U **Unconditional election** – The true Calvinist believes God
chooses to save some people, not because of anything of
merit they have done but rather, according to His sovereign
will. Some Calvinists take this to the extent that God elects
some to eternal punishment. While this is logical, many
would not advance this position knowing God's sovereign
will does not have to line up with our logic. Clearly such a
view (called double election) is a major distinguishing view
from those who believe God desires all to be saved and that
Christ died for all to come to salvation, but that God elects
those He foreknows will respond to His grace.

Other verses relating to unconditional election are: "When
the Gentiles heard this, they were glad and honored the
word of the Lord; and all who were appointed for eternal life

believed" (Acts 13:48). "Therefore God has mercy on whom he wants to have mercy, and he hardens whom he wants to harden" (Romans 9:18). "For he chose us in him before the creation of the world to be holy and blameless in his sight. In love he predestined us to be adopted as his sons through Jesus Christ, in accordance with his pleasure and will" (Ephesians 1:4-5).

L **Limited atonement** – This part of the Calvinist position states Christ died for the elect (those who come to faith in Him) and not for the whole world. "For even the Son of Man did not come to be served, but to serve, and to give his life as a ransom for many" (Mark 10:45). Note: a critic of Calvinism can easily say the "many" means all who will come to Christ, not just to the predetermined. "No one can come to me unless the Father who sent me draws him" (John 6:44). "…we preach Christ crucified: a stumbling block to Jews and foolishness to Gentiles, but to those whom God has called, both Jews and Greeks, Christ the power of God and the wisdom of God" (1 Corinthians 1:23-24).

I **Irresistible grace** – This teaches that if God elects a person to salvation that person cannot resist the drawing of the Holy Spirit to salvation. God never loses. The words "free will" are not in the Scriptures as related to salvation. If God has elected a person to salvation, His election and call are irresistible. A New Testament example is Lydia. "One of those listening was a woman named Lydia, a dealer in purple cloth from the city of Thyatira, who was a worshiper of God. The Lord opened her heart to respond to Paul's message" (Acts 16:14). This view is in contrast to some Arminians that believe while God may choose to save everyone, not everyone chooses to believe.

P **Perseverance of the saints** – This means that when a person comes in faith to God, this believer will endure to the end. "I give them eternal life, and they shall never perish; no one can snatch them out of my hand. My Father, who has given them to me, is greater than all; no one can snatch them out of my Father's hand. I and the Father are one" (John 10:28-30). "And those he predestined, he also called; those he called, he also justified; those he justified, he also glorified" (Romans 8:30). "…being confident of this, that he who began a good work in you will carry it on to completion until the day of Christ Jesus" (Philippians 1:6). In opposition to this view is another Christian tradition which teaches people can forsake faith and thus lose their salvation.

There are places in Scripture that I cannot reconcile with Calvinism, such as: "But there were also false prophets among the people, just as there will be false teachers among you. They will secretly introduce destructive heresies, even denying the sovereign Lord who bought them—bringing swift destruction on themselves" (2 Peter 2:1). Here are people who were "false prophets." "They will secretly introduce destructive heresies, *even denying the sovereign Lord who bought them*—bringing swift destruction on themselves" (emphasis mine). Christ died for these people. One of the tenets of Calvinism is "limited atonement," which means Christ died only for the elect. Here it states He died for some who were apparently not of the elect. If they were of the elect, they would have come to Christ because, as mentioned before, God never loses. On the cross, Jesus died for them. Second Corinthians says that He "died for all." If Christ only died for the elect, what do we do with 2 Corinthians 5:14 where it says: "For Christ's love compels us, because we are convinced that one died for all." Does "all" mean "all"? I have never heard a true Calvinist give a credible integration of this verse into his or her view of Calvinism. Verses like 2 Peter 2:1 and 2 Corinthians 5:14, where it says Christ died for all, give me pause.

There is a surge of Calvinism at this time, seemingly among younger pastors, though not exclusively with them. Although previously more inclined toward the Arminian perspective, they continue to come into the verses on our being chosen and predestined and are saying, "There's something to this. God is saying something I have been missing over the years."

Arminianism

Typically Arminians believe that one can lose their salvation and be saved over and over. They also speak a lot about "free will." Interestingly, as mentioned in Chapter 9, this is not a New Testament phrase related to salvation. That by itself does not rule out "free will." The word "Trinity" is not in the Bible and yet we know by looking at all of Scripture there is a Holy Trinity of God the Father, God the Son, and God the Holy Spirit. We know from Scripture that each one of them is God and yet there is only one God. Thus, we believe in the Trinity.

Arminianism is named for Jacob Arminius. He and his followers believed Christ died for all rather than just for the elect.

The following are the 24 tenets of the Arminian theology according to *Baker's Dictionary of Theology* (© 1966, used by permission of Baker Academic, a division of Baker Publishing Group):

1. God's knowledge of the future acts of free agents is to mediate. (I find this difficult to understand—a Thesaurus gives other verbs such as "arbitrate," "intercede," "referee," "intervene," "reconcile," "act as a go-between" and, for an antonym, uses the word "provoke").

2. God's decrees are based on His foreknowledge: election on foreseen faith and reprobation on foreseen resistance to grace.

3. The image of God in man consists in man's dominion over the lower creation.

4. Adam was created in innocence rather than in true holiness.

5. The covenant of works was abrogated after the Fall.

6. Sin consists in acts of the will.

7. Pollution is inherited from Adam, but his guilt is not imputed to any of his descendants.

8. Man's depravity as a result of the Fall should not be described as total.

9. Man has not lost the faculty of self-determination nor the ability to incline his will toward good ends.

10. The atonement was not absolutely necessary, but represents merely one way that God chose among man to manifest His love without prejudice to His righteousness.

11. The atonement is intended equally for all men and for every man, and it merely makes salvation possible. Salvation becomes effectual only when accepted by the repentant believer.

12. There is no common grace to be distinguished from special grace.

13. The external call of the gospel is accompanied by a universal sufficient grace that can be resisted.

14. Repentance and faith precede regeneration.

15. The human will is to be viewed as one of the causes of regeneration (synergism).

16. Faith is a good work of man and a ground of acceptance with God.

17. There is no imputation of Christ's righteousness to the believer.

18. The believer is able to attain in this life a state of such

conformity to the Divine will that he may be called perfect.

19. As long as a man lives, he may fall away from grace and lose his salvation altogether.

20. Love is the supreme attribute of God, the very essence of His being.

21. The goal of creation is the happiness of the creatures (eudaemonism).

22. Man was created naturally mortal.

23. The atonement is not strictly substitutionary and penal, but it is a token performance designed to safeguard the interests of the moral government of God while opening the possibility of salvation on the basis of evangelical obedience (rectorial or governmental theory of the atonement).

24. Assurance of salvation is not possible in this life, except by a special personal revelation.

I, like many of you, have spoken with people who call themselves Calvinists and others who call themselves Arminians. Only a minority of either group would probably subscribe to all the tenets of their position. We are closer together than our labels have allowed us to believe.

There is often wholesome debate between those who hold to the Calvinist and Arminian positions. There are often misconceptions and logical misunderstandings (our logic, not God's

Word) of the two theological positions and within these positions. For example, I have frequently heard criticism of the position of eternal salvation (or eternal security or perseverance of
the saints) that is worded similar to the following: "That means
you can accept Christ as Savior and Lord and then live your
life in sin and you will still end up in heaven." Earlier I quoted
my dad (he believed in the perseverance of the saints) as saying: "Regardless of your theology, you can't live like the devil on
earth and go to heaven when you die." Another misconception
of the Calvinist position and within the Calvinist position relates
to world missions and reaching out in evangelism. Using human
logic, not God's Word, it goes along the lines of: "If God predestines people to salvation and they are the only ones who can be
saved, and they will be saved, why do we send out missionaries
and work hard at local outreach?" There is one very simple and
conclusive answer. God told us to seek the lost locally, region-
ally, and across the world. Romans 10:14-15 says: "How, then,
can they call on the one they have not believed in? And how can
they believe in the one of whom they have not heard? And how
can they hear without someone preaching to them? And how
can they preach unless they are sent?" Further, "...you will be
my witnesses in Jerusalem, and in all Judea and Samaria, and
to the ends of the earth" (Acts 1:8) was the final recorded command of Christ before He ascended.

One of the reasons people are drawn from Calvinism and
lean to the Arminian position is because of the "L" of TULIP
(Limited Atonement). They do not find it palatable to accept
that when Jesus died, He died for the elect rather than dying for
the salvation of all people. There are questions on other parts as
well. However, the purpose of this Appendix is to let you know

what the Calvinist and Arminian positions are—not to say all Calvinists and all Arminians hold to the historical positions. The views of those calling themselves Calvinists or Arminians are often not as far apart in our generation as described here. It generally boils down to a few major issues for each group. For many Calvinists, it is the issue of a secure, eternal salvation that only happens as the Holy Spirit draws us to Christ. They also lean towards a strong belief in God superintending the affairs of this world. It is good to remember some of the greatest evangelistic efforts today are by those who hold more to the Arminian position. It is also fair to applaud those in the Holiness Movement for aiming at holiness of living while our plea is they not claim it as having completely arrived (1 John 1:8).

Perhaps some readers who thought they were Arminians may now say, "I guess I'm not." Others who thought they were Calvinists may be saying, "I guess I'm not." Perhaps you are a blend of both. With respect for systematic theology's great contribution to biblical understanding, I find myself more comfortable (and not trying to be overly pious here) letting the Bible speak for itself; understanding there are things we will not understand this side of heaven. There are scriptural passages and doctrinal issues that we cannot put together in neat columns, even though we believe every word of Scripture. This would fit the earlier reference to Deuteronomy 29:29: "The secret things belong to the Lord our God," as well as Paul's writing about the "unsearchable riches of Christ" (Ephesians 3:8). I am well aware Paul was speaking to people who did not have the New Testament and, therefore, some unsearchable things to them are searchable to us. However, there are areas, even with our having both the Old and New Testaments, that defy conclusive understanding.

Index of Scripture Verses
(in Bible book order)

Index of Scripture Verses
(in Bible book order)

Index of Scripture Verses
(in Bible book order)

Book of the Bible .... Page Number

New Testament

Index of Scripture Verses
(in Bible book order)

Index of Scripture Verses
(in Bible book order)

Index of Scripture Verses
(in Bible book order)

Index of Scripture Verses
(in Bible book order)

Index of Scripture Verses
(in Bible book order)

Index of Scripture Verses
(in Bible book order)

Index of Scripture Verses
(in Bible book order)